D1385400

Should Abortion Be Legal?

Carla Mooney

INCONTROVERSY

ReferencePoint Press®

San Diego, CA

© 2014 ReferencePoint Press, Inc.
Printed in the United States

For more information, contact:
ReferencePoint Press, Inc.
PO Box 27779
San Diego, CA 92198
www. ReferencePointPress.com

LIBRARY OF CONGRESS CATALOGING-IN-PUBLICATION DATA

Mooney, Carla, 1970– author.
  Should abortion be legal? / By Carla Mooney.
    pages cm. -- (In controversy)
  Includes bibliographical references and index.
  ISBN-13: 978-1-60152-624-3 (hardback)
  ISBN-10: 1-60152-624-5 (hardback)
1. Abortion--Law and legislation--United States. I. Title.
  KF3771.M66   2013
  342.7308'4--dc23
                                                                2013032608

Contents

Foreword

In 2008, as the US economy and economies worldwide were falling into the worst recession since the Great Depression, most Americans had difficulty comprehending the complexity, magnitude, and scope of what was happening. As is often the case with a complex, controversial issue such as this historic global economic recession, looking at the problem as a whole can be overwhelming and often does not lead to understanding. One way to better comprehend such a large issue or event is to break it into smaller parts. The intricacies of global economic recession may be difficult to understand, but one can gain insight by instead beginning with an individual contributing factor, such as the real estate market. When examined through a narrower lens, complex issues become clearer and easier to evaluate.

This is the idea behind ReferencePoint Press's *In Controversy* series. The series examines the complex, controversial issues of the day by breaking them into smaller pieces. Rather than looking at the stem cell research debate as a whole, a title would examine an important aspect of the debate such as *Is Stem Cell Research Necessary?* or *Is Embryonic Stem Cell Research Ethical?* By studying the central issues of the debate individually, researchers gain a more solid and focused understanding of the topic as a whole.

Each book in the series provides a clear, insightful discussion of the issues, integrating facts and a variety of contrasting opinions for a solid, balanced perspective. Personal accounts and direct quotes from academic and professional experts, advocacy groups, politicians, and others enhance the narrative. Sidebars add depth to the discussion by expanding on important ideas and events. For quick reference, a list of key facts concludes every chapter. Source notes, an annotated organizations list, bibliography, and index provide student researchers with additional tools for papers and class discussion.

The *In Controversy* series also challenges students to think critically about issues, to improve their problem-solving skills, and to sharpen their ability to form educated opinions. As President Barack Obama stated in a March 2009 speech, success in the twenty-first century will not be measurable merely by students' ability to "fill in a bubble on a test but whether they possess 21st century skills like problem-solving and critical thinking and entrepreneurship and creativity." Those who possess these skills will have a strong foundation for whatever lies ahead.

No one can know for certain what sort of world awaits today's students. What we can assume, however, is that those who are inquisitive about a wide range of issues; open-minded to divergent views; aware of bias and opinion; and able to reason, reflect, and reconsider will be best prepared for the future. As the international development organization Oxfam notes, "Today's young people will grow up to be the citizens of the future: but what that future holds for them is uncertain. We can be quite confident, however, that they will be faced with decisions about a wide range of issues on which people have differing, contradictory views. If they are to develop as global citizens all young people should have the opportunity to engage with these controversial issues."

In Controversy helps today's students better prepare for tomorrow. An understanding of the complex issues that drive our world and the ability to think critically about them are essential components of contributing, competing, and succeeding in the twenty-first century.

Clashing Beliefs

I n January 2013, seventy-year old antiabortion activist Joyce Fecteau was arrested in Huntsville, Alabama, in front of the Alabama Women's Center for Reproductive Alternatives. She was charged with misdemeanor harassment. Fecteau and other antiabortion protesters are often on the sidewalk outside the Alabama Women's Center on Wednesdays and Saturdays, when the clinic performs abortions. Some of the protesters try to talk to women entering the clinic, while others pray loudly, wave signs, or hand out antiabortion brochures.

On this particular day police arrested Fecteau in connection with an incident that had occurred the previous month. Abortion rights demonstrator Lisa Cox had sworn out a warrant accusing Fecteau of spraying her in the face with an unknown substance. In April 2013 a municipal court judge found Fecteau not guilty of harassment.

Heated Feelings about Abortion

The case is an example of the heated feelings in the years-long national debate over abortion and how that debate plays out daily in people's lives. At the clinic in Huntsville women who come there for services of all types, not just abortions, must maneuver past the antiabortion protesters just to get in the door. In response, abortion rights activists in Huntsville have organized volunteers to provide escorts for women seeking care at the clinic. Volunteers park the patient's car and escort her into the clinic, providing a human shield against protesters. Pro-choice activists have also set up competing demonstrations outside the clinic, challenging the antiabortion protesters with their own signs and pro-choice messages. Both sides believe strongly that their actions are justified.

Antiabortion protesters believe that if they can convince even one woman to change her mind about getting an abortion, then they have succeeded. When asked if such actions violated the privacy of the clinic's patients, one antiabortion protester speaking anonymously responded, "If they can't feel any regard to the life that they are ending, then I feel protesting is needed to wake up their conscience. . . . I support women's rights, but I also support life. As a Christian woman, abortion goes against everything that I stand for."[1]

Abortion rights advocates believe just as strongly that the antiabortion protesters are violating the privacy of women coming to the clinic for services that are legal and a matter of personal choice. "I think governments should develop a buffer zone policy that will ensure protestors can exercise their right to organize and have free speech while allowing patients to have access to this legal procedure without fear or intimidation,"[2] says Amanda Reyes, a pro-choice volunteer escort for the West Alabama Women's Center in Tuscaloosa, Alabama.

In 2013 in Washington DC, protesters on both sides of the abortion issue mark the 40th anniversary of the Roe v. Wade *decision that legalized abortion in the United States. Polls show that Americans continue to have mixed feelings about abortion.*

Opposing Sides

As illustrated by the conflict between pro-life and pro-choice groups at abortion clinics all across country, the issue of abortion continues to divide Americans. In 1973 the US Supreme Court decided *Roe v. Wade*, a landmark case that gave women the constitutional right to a legal abortion. Rather than settling the issue, however, the ruling set off more debate. Many people feel passionate about abortion—either that it should be legal and always left up to each individual woman or that it is murder and should not be allowed under any circumstances.

Recent polls reveal that Americans are, for the most part, less strident than either of these positions suggests. When a May 2013 Gallup poll asked participants if they considered themselves pro-choice or pro-life, the results were fairly even with 45 percent of respondents identifying themselves as pro-choice and 48 percent describing themselves as pro-life. Yet, according to a 2013 *Wall Street Journal*/NBC poll, 70 percent of Americans support keeping abortion legal. These results reflect that most Americans hold complex views on abortion. They struggle to find a fair way to balance the rights of the woman and the unborn child. "While there are very well organized and very ideological pro-life and pro-choice groups, your average citizen is in neither of these groups. He or she is in the middle,"[3] says Tom W. Smith, head of the General Social Survey at the University of Chicago's National Opinion Research Center, which has been tracking public sentiment on abortion since 1972.

An individual's position on abortion is often rooted in his or her personal beliefs about religion, ethics, personal freedom, family, and other issues. Whether pro-life or pro-choice, both sides believe that they are justified in their beliefs, defending those whose rights are being unfairly denied. As a result, the debate over abortion continues to be as heated and emotional today as in the past.

"While there are very well organized and very ideological pro-life and pro-choice groups, your average citizen is in neither of these groups. He or she is in the middle."[3]

— Tom W. Smith, head of the General Social Survey at the University of Chicago's National Opinion Research Center.

Facts

- At least half of American women will experience an unintended pregnancy by age 45, and 1 in 10 women will have an abortion by age 20, 1 in 4 by age 30, and 3 in 10 by age 45, according to the Guttmacher Institute.

- According to the Guttmacher Institute, 22 percent of all pregnancies, excluding miscarriages, end in abortion.

- Two kinds of abortion are available in the United States—an in-clinic abortion and use of the abortion pill.

- The National Right to Life Committee estimates that approximately 1.2 million abortions occur in the United States annually.

What Are the Origins of the Abortion Controversy?

In March 1970 a twenty-one-year-old woman from Dallas County, Texas, filed a class-action lawsuit against Henry Wade, the Dallas County district attorney. The woman, known by the pseudonym Jane Roe, wanted to have a legal abortion in Texas. In the *Roe v. Wade* lawsuit Roe's attorneys claimed that the Texas statues that restricted abortion were unconstitutional and violated Roe's right to personal privacy. While the Texas courts ruled that Roe's claim had merit, they refused to issue an injunction against the law that banned abortion. Roe's lawyers appealed the decision, and by 1972 the lawsuit reached the US Supreme Court.

Historic Ruling

After hearing testimony in the case, the Supreme Court issued its groundbreaking decision on January 22, 1973. The justices voted seven to two in favor of *Roe*, granting American women the constitutional right to have an abortion. The majority of the justices based their decision on the reasoning that denying a woman an abortion violated her right to privacy under the US Constitution's Fourteenth Amendment. The Fourteenth Amendment states in part: "No state shall make or enforce any law which shall abridge the privileges or immunities of citizens of the United States; nor shall any state deprive any person of life, liberty, or property, without due process of law; nor deny to any person within its jurisdiction the equal protection of the laws."[4]

The justices decided that during the early stages of pregnancy a woman had the right to decide if she will bear a child. Chief Justice Harry Blackmun writes in the court's majority opinion that the "right of privacy, whether it be founded in the Fourteenth Amendment's concept of personal liberty and restrictions upon state action, as we feel it is . . . is broad enough to encompass a woman's decision whether or not to terminate her pregnancy."[5]

In the decision the court set up a framework to guide abortion regulation based on the three trimesters of a woman's pregnancy. During the first trimester (week 1 through week 12) a woman's right to privacy is the strongest and therefore the states should not regulate abortion for any reason. During the second trimester (week 13 through week 26) state regulation should be permitted only to protect a woman's health. In the third trimester (week 27 to birth), the state's interest in the potential life of the fetus becomes stronger, allowing states to regulate or ban abortion except in cases where it was needed to save a woman's life or protect her from serious physical harm.

> "[The] right of privacy . . . is broad enough to encompass a woman's decision whether or not to terminate her pregnancy."[5]
>
> — Harry Blackmun, Chief Justice of the US Supreme Court, 1973.

Doe v. Bolton Ruling

On the same day, the court also ruled on a related case, *Doe v. Bolton*, which challenged Georgia abortion restrictions that permitted abortion only in cases of rape, severe fetal deformity, or severe maternal injury. The Georgia restrictions also required abortions to be performed only in accredited hospitals after review by a hospital committee and an exam by two doctors, not including the woman's personal doctor. The Supreme Court struck down these restrictions, with the same seven to two majority.

In both cases the same two justices, Byron White and William Rehnquist, dissented with the majority opinion. They argued that by nullifying state abortion laws the court had exceeded its constitutional powers. In his dissent in the *Doe v. Bolton* case, White writes,

I find nothing in the language or history of the Constitution to support the Court's judgment. The Court simply fashions and announces a new constitutional right for pregnant mothers and, with scarcely any reason or authority for its action, invests that right with sufficient substance to override most existing state abortion statutes . . . in my view its judgment is an improvident and extravagant exercise of the power of judicial review that the Constitution extends to this Court. The Court apparently values the convenience of the pregnant mother more than the continued existence and development of the life or potential life that she carries.[6]

Effects of the Supreme Court Rulings

The *Roe v. Wade* and *Doe v. Bolton* rulings had an immediate impact across the country. For the first time in American history, women had the legal option to decide whether they wanted to continue a pregnancy. "Prior to *Roe*, whether one could obtain a legal abortion in the face of an unwanted pregnancy was a crapshoot. For 40 years now, it's been a constitutionally guaranteed right,"[7] says David Garrow, a Supreme Court scholar and University of Pittsburgh law professor. The rulings affected laws in forty-six states, where many restrictions on abortion were struck down as unconstitutional.

Although the court's decision legalized abortion, the issue was far from settled. The majority opinion acknowledged that the states have a legitimate interest in protecting the health of their citizens, in setting standards of medical care, and in safeguarding potential life. Blackmun writes that the right to privacy "is not absolute and is subject to some limitations; and that at some point the state interests as to protection of health, medical standards, and prenatal life, become dominant."[8] This statement has been interpreted

Signs in the crowd read: "LOVE LIFE", "I am glad I was born", "ABORTION", "EVERYONE SHOULD HAVE A BIRTHDAY", "I'm GLAD "YOU" WERE BORN", "EVERYONE SHOULD HAVE A BIRTHDAY", "JANUARY 22, 1973 Blackest Day In U.S. History", "LET US", "A CHILD"

over the years as justification for imposing certain restrictions on abortion. Yet the court also required the states to justify any such restrictions by showing that they have a compelling interest in doing so. Rather than ending the controversy, the Supreme Court's 1973 rulings added more fuel to the long-running national debate on abortion.

As news of the Supreme Court's abortion ruling spread, protesters who opposed legal abortion took to the streets. One such rally took place in St. Paul, Minnesota (pictured), on January 22, 1973, the day the court issued its groundbreaking decision.

Early Dangers Lead to Bans

The controversy over abortion had been brewing for decades. In the late 1700s abortions were commonly performed before quickening, the time when a pregnant woman can feel fetal movements. Midwives, apothecaries, and homeopaths—many of whom lacked medical training—often performed the procedures. Depending on the skill of the provider, abortions could be dangerous and sometimes deadly for women.

To prevent untrained practitioners from performing abortions, doctors led a campaign in the 1800s to criminalize abortion except in rare cases where it was needed to save a pregnant woman's life. In 1812 Connecticut became the first state to pass a law that banned abortion after quickening. In 1857 the American Medical Association (AMA) created a Committee on Criminal Abortion. The Committee presented a report at the AMA's 1859 annual meeting, recommending that the AMA request states and territories to implement laws against abortion. The AMA also asked state medical societies to lobby for antiabortion laws. These efforts were successful, and by 1910 almost every state had passed laws to ban abortion, with limited exceptions.

Faced with an unplanned pregnancy, women during this period had two options. They could either have the child or go to someone who could help them end the pregnancy. In some cases these women were poor and could not afford to feed or clothe another child. Others were unmarried and fearful of the social stigma of becoming an unwed mother. During the late 1800s and early 1900s, unwed mothers and their children frequently were shunned by their families and communities. Rather than having to face disapproval and judgment from friends and neighbors, many parents sent pregnant teenagers to remote homes for unwed mothers to have their babies in secret. These scared, young mothers were often forced to give up their babies for adoption because they had no income or means of support outside of their families. With few options, desperate pregnant women sought out ways to terminate an unwanted pregnancy despite state laws banning the procedure.

Abortions Done in Secret

Some women obtained relatively safe abortions from doctors who were willing to defy the law. But these doctors also faced increased pressure from their peers and from hospital administrators to stop doing illegal abortions. Doctors could be fined, serve jail time, and lose their medical license if convicted of performing a criminal abortion. In Texas, where abortion was criminalized in 1854, a

"Prior to Roe, whether one could obtain a legal abortion in the face of an unwanted pregnancy was a crapshoot. For 40 years now, it's been a constitutionally guaranteed right."[7]

— David Garrow, law professor at the University of Pittsburgh and Supreme Court scholar.

Roe v. Wade's Trimester Analysis

In its *Roe v. Wade* ruling, the Supreme Court concluded that women had a constitutional right to abortion but that states had an important interest in protecting the mother's health and the potential of human life she carried. Justice Harry Blackmun created a three-tiered legal framework, based on pregnancy's three trimesters to guide state abortion regulation.

The first tier covers the first trimester of pregnancy. Blackmun states that because the health risks involved in having an abortion during this period are minimal, the state has little interest in limiting abortion at this stage. Therefore, states could not limit access to abortion during this period but could require that it be performed by a qualified health professional.

The framework's second tier covers the second trimester of pregnancy to the point of fetal viability, usually between twenty-four to twenty-eight weeks as determined by the woman's doctor. During this period, Blackmun writes, the state could only regulate abortion to protect the health of the mother. Any state regulations could not be aimed at protecting the fetus or limiting abortion access.

The third tier covers the pregnancy after fetal viability. During this time, Blackmun determined that the state had an interest in protecting the life of the fetus. States could ban abortion during this time, with exceptions that allowed the procedure to protect the life and health of the mother.

person convicted of helping a pregnant woman procure an abortion faced a punishment of two to five years imprisonment. In addition, anyone convicted of attempting to procure an abortion faced a fine of $100 to $1,000. Over time, many doctors did stop performing abortions.

As a result, the number of abortions done by private doctors declined, and more women turned to unqualified practitioners—or tried to end their pregnancies on their own. The National Abortion Federation, which supports legal abortion, estimates that illegal abortions were as high as 1.2 million per year in the 1950s and 1960s. The abortion providers were often unqualified to perform medical procedures and worked in unsanitary facilities, which put the women at risk for infection and disease. Many women suffered serious medical harm, became infertile, or even died from botched procedures. Hospital emergency rooms treated thousands of women who suffered serious complications from unsafe abortions.

Gynecologist Mildred Hanson witnessed the devastating effects of illegal abortion before *Roe v. Wade.* "I found myself becoming angry that women had to accept an unwanted pregnancy," she says. "I was frustrated that there was such an easy thing to do that was within our grasp technically, and yet we were denying it to women, and women were dying because of it. It seemed so unconscionable that we, as doctors, were allowing this to happen, when there clearly was an easy, efficient, cost-effective, safe procedure to terminate unwanted pregnancies. Instead, we were putting women through all this trauma, putting their lives on the line and making them endure unwanted pregnancies. It just didn't make sense."[9]

Calls for Legal Abortion

By the mid-twentieth century calls for legalized abortion emerged. Some of the first supporters of legalizing abortion came from the medical profession and a prominent group of judges and lawyers called the American Law Institute. "These were . . . professional organizations that looked at the regime of criminal abortion laws that were driving women to back alleys and were putting doctors in legal jeopardy if they acted in what they considered to be the best interests of their patients, and that's where the impetus for change really began,"[10] says Linda Greenhouse of Yale Law School. Groups of doctors and lawyers argued that medicine, not the law, should regulate abortion so that women facing extremely difficult pregnancies could have access to a qualified provider and a safe, sanitary procedure. Medical technology and hospitals had advanced so that the procedure could be performed relatively safely by trained staff

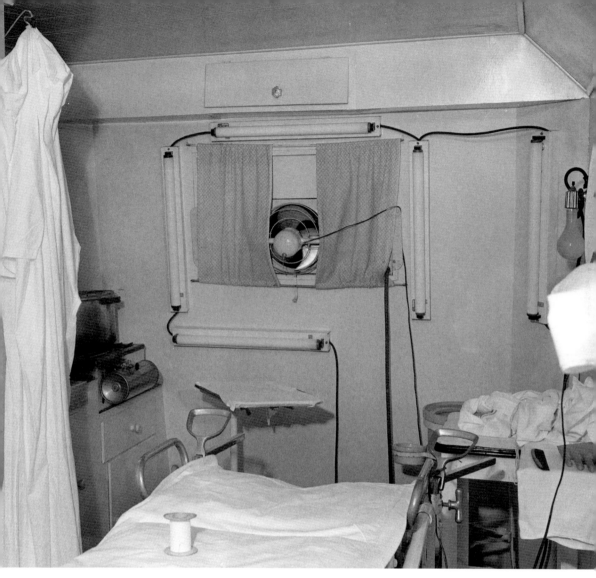

in clean facilities. These groups argued that it was time to rewrite the state laws that made almost every abortion illegal.

As the abortion rights movement took hold, several states changed their abortion laws. In 1967 Colorado became the first state to expand the circumstances under which a woman could obtain a legal abortion. The new Colorado statute allowed abortion if the pregnant woman's life or physical or mental health was in danger, in cases of severe physical or mental defect of the fetus, and in cases of rape or incest. By the end of 1972 thirteen states had made similar changes to their abortion laws. Four states, New

Before abortion became legal, women who sought to end their pregnancies often turned to unsafe, unsanitary, and untrained practitioners for help. Pictured is the inside of a trailer in which abortions were performed in 1948.

York, Washington, Hawaii, and Alaska, repealed their antiabortion laws entirely, permitting abortion if determined necessary by a woman and her doctor. Several states allowed abortion only in cases of rape and incest, to protect the health of the pregnant woman, or because of a fetal abnormality. Mississippi, for example, allowed abortion only in cases of rape and incest, while Alabama allowed the procedure to save a woman's life or prevent serious and irreversible damage to a major bodily function. Thirty-one states allowed abortion only to save the mother's life. "Between 1967 and 1970, a total of 19 states had legalized abortion for reasons other than to save the life of the mother,"[11] says David O'Steen, executive director of the National Right to Life Committee, an antiabortion organization.

As the abortion rights movement gained momentum, several organizations emerged as advocates and lobbyists. Today, Planned Parenthood, NARAL Pro-Choice America, the National Organization for Women, and the American Civil Liberties Union (ACLU) are active at the state and federal levels. Members of these groups campaign for legal abortion and protest the passage of antiabortion laws.

Antiabortion Movement

As efforts to change abortion laws increased around the country, people who opposed abortion began to organize their own movement. The first statewide antiabortion group, the Virginia Society of Human Life, formed in 1967. It was soon followed by the formation of antiabortion groups in several other states.

The Catholic Church joined this movement, becoming a prominent voice in opposing reform of abortion laws. "In the mid '60s, the pope instructed the U.S. bishops to make abortion a priority. And they did,"[12] says Jon O'Brien, president of the abortion rights group Catholics for Choice. In 1970 the National Conference of Catholic Bishops issued a declaration on abortion, stating that "The child in the womb is human. Abortion is an unjust destruction of a human life, and morally that is murder. Society has no right to destroy this life. Even the expectant mother has no such right. The law must establish every possible protection for the child before and after birth."[13] The church battled reform efforts in numerous states, including New York. In 1970, for example, that state's legislature passed a bill that removed all restrictions on abortion in the first twenty-four weeks of pregnancy. Thousands of Catholic antiabortion protesters flocked to Albany, the capital of New York State. By 1972 pressure from the church and protesters

Several organizations emerged as vocal advocates for the differing views in the abortion debate. Planned Parenthood, founded in 1916 in connection with the opening of the nation's first birth control clinic, is a strong proponent of abortion rights.

forced a vote in the New York legislature to reinstate the old law. Although the legislature voted to revoke the law that repealed the abortion ban, New York governor Nelson Rockefeller vetoed the bill, effectively leaving New York's abortion law in force.

When the Supreme Court issued its January 1973 ruling in *Roe v. Wade*, state antiabortion groups saw the need for a national effort to respond to the ruling. In May the National Right to Life Committee (NRLC) incorporated, and thirty state groups elected representatives for a national board of directors. The group, which received some of its funding from the National Conference of Catholic Bishops, opened its national office in Washington, DC, later that same year. Since its formation, the NRLC has become the largest antiabortion organization in the United States, with affiliates in every state and more than three thousand local chapters.

After *Roe v. Wade*

The *Roe* ruling became one of the most controversial decisions handed down in Supreme Court history. Before the ruling no federal law regulated abortion. States could regulate abortion as they saw fit. That changed with the Supreme Court's decision. Because the court determined that a woman's right to an abortion was protected under the Constitution, any state laws that banned abortion could be found unconstitutional and overturned on appeal. Although some agreed with the court's position, others believed it had overstepped its bounds and misinterpreted whether abortion is a constitutional right.

In the years after *Roe* the Supreme Court upheld a woman's right to an abortion in several cases. In 1976 the court struck down a Missouri law that required a woman to obtain her husband's consent for a first-trimester abortion. In 1990 the court ruled against a Minnesota law that required women under age eighteen to notify both parents before obtaining an abortion. The court also struck down regulations that required women to be informed about the risks of the procedure and then undergo a twenty-four-hour waiting period.

The Supreme Court has also upheld state laws that the justices felt did not significantly limit a woman's right to end her pregnancy. In 1989, for instance, the court sided with Missouri in *Webster v.*

Reproductive Health Services. At issue in that case was a Missouri law passed in the 1980s banning government doctors and state employees from performing or assisting with abortions unless the mother's life was in danger. The law also stated that public funds and state facilities could not be used for abortion procedures. The statute defined life as beginning at conception and instructed doctors to perform tests of fetal viability, the point at which a fetus can survive outside the womb, at twenty-four weeks gestation, the age of the fetus from conception. In a five to four decision the court upheld the Missouri law, finding that it did not violate a woman's right to obtain an abortion. The justices ruled that the *Roe* decision did not give the federal government the right to force states to make funds and facilities available for abortions. The majority also ruled that viability testing at twenty-four weeks gestation was constitutional.

State Restrictions on Abortion

In recent years, as the makeup of the court's justices has become more conservative, the court has been more willing to uphold some state restrictions on abortions. In 1992 the Supreme Court heard *Planned Parenthood v. Casey*, a case that challenged parts of a Pennsylvania law that imposed conditions on abortion. The state law required doctors to inform women seeking abortion about the risks of the procedure and imposed a twenty-four-hour waiting period. The statute required minors seeking an abortion to have the consent of at least one parent or guardian. It also required spousal notification, whereby a wife was required to inform her husband of her intent to end a pregnancy.

In its ruling the court affirmed *Roe*'s core principle—that women had the right to obtain abortions before viability. The justices also struck down the Pennsylvania law's spousal notification provision. Yet they upheld the Pennsylvania statute's other restrictions, reasoning that these requirements did not impose an undue burden on women and were within Pennsylvania's rights and interests.

While the ruling maintained the legality of abortion under *Roe* and solidified it as legal precedent, which would make it harder for future challenges to overturn it, the court's ruling also opened the door for states to regulate abortion during the entire pregnancy. *Roe*'s trimester framework had prohibited regulation of abortion during the first trimester and limited regulation between the end of the first trimester and fetal viability. After *Casey*, states could regulate abortion throughout a woman's pregnancy. In addition, the *Casey* ruling created a new standard for determining whether state abortion laws were constitutional. In *Roe v. Wade*, the court stated that states could only regulate abortion if there was a compelling state interest. In the years after *Roe*, many state regulations were struck down as unconstitutional based on this strict standard. In *Casey*, the court used a less strict undue burden standard. Using this guide, a state abortion regulation was considered unconstitutional only if it imposed an undue burden on the woman's right to end her pregnancy.

The court again upheld abortion rights when it struck down a Nebraska ban on partial-birth abortions in June 2000. Partial-birth

"*Abortion is just a different kind of issue, even for those who support it. It's not the kind of issue that one celebrates.*"[15]

— Robert P. Jones, chief executive of the Public Religion Research Institute.

abortions were defined under the law as any abortion in which the fetus was partially delivered before it was aborted. The court overturned the law, ruling that it created an undue burden on women seeking an abortion because it could be applied to abortions other than late-term procedures. The court ruled that Nebraska doctors should be able to use their own expertise and judgment in determining how to perform an abortion and that a law should not make this determination for them. Because of this ruling, similar laws in thirty other states were invalidated. The court would later revisit the issue and reverse its position in 2007.

The Debate Today

Decades after *Roe v. Wade* the abortion debate remains heated. Advocates on both sides of the issue continue to fight over the legality of abortion, and who should have the right to determine its legal status. "As long as there are really vocal minorities that regard [abortion] as the most important issue in our lifetime, and some of them do, there will be attempts to get it on the agenda,"[14] says Morris Fiorina, a political scientist and senior fellow of the Hoover Institution at Stanford University. In addition, both sides are watching the justices on the Supreme Court, knowing that any change to the court's makeup could affect future rulings on abortion.

Despite the ongoing debate, American attitudes about abortion have been stable since the 1970s, says Ted G. Jelen, a professor of political science at the University of Nevada, Las Vegas. According to the survey organization American National Election Studies (ANES), 11 percent of Americans in 1972 said that abortions should never be permitted, a number that is only slightly lower than the 15 percent of Americans in 2008 who expressed the same view. In addition, support for legal abortion has remained constant over several decades. According to a 2013 poll by the Pew Research Center, 63 percent of respondents do not want the Supreme Court to overturn *Roe v. Wade*, as compared to 62 percent in 2003 and 60 percent in 1993.

Despite the passage of time, abortion remains a divisive, complex, and emotional issue. "Abortion is just a different kind of issue, even for those who support it," says Robert P. Jones, chief executive of the Public Religion Research Institute, a nonprofit organization that studies religion and public life. "It's not the kind of issue that one celebrates."[15]

Facts

- An estimated sixty-eight thousand women worldwide die each year from unsafe abortions performed in countries where abortion is illegal, reports the National Abortion Federation.

- Congress has barred the use of federal Medicaid funds to pay for abortions except when the woman's life would be endangered by a full-term pregnancy or in cases of rape or incest.

- Abortion is one of the safest medical procedures, with less than 0.5 percent risk of major complications, according to the National Abortion Federation.

- According to the CDC, at least 44.7 percent of the women who had abortions in 2009 had obtained at least one previous abortion. At least 19.5 percent of women who aborted had at least two previous abortions.

- According to the Center for Reproductive Rights, 74 countries permit abortion on broad grounds or without restriction as to reason.

Is Abortion Moral?

At the core of the abortion debate is the central question: is abortion moral? The answer is often determined by an individual's personal beliefs about religion, ethics, personal freedom, and other issues. Some people believe that the fetus is a human being with full moral status and rights from conception. Others believe that a fetus has no rights, even if it is human in a biological sense. Most Americans' beliefs fall somewhere in between the two extremes.

Public Opinion: Legal Versus Moral

Although abortion is a hotly debated issue, support for legal abortion remains high among American adults. In a January 2013 poll conducted by the *Wall Street Journal* (WSJ) and NBC, seven in ten Americans said they thought the Supreme Court's *Roe v. Wade* decision that legalized abortion should stand. This was the highest level of support for the *Roe* decision since the polls began tracking it in 1989.

While Americans overwhelmingly support keeping abortion legal, they have mixed feelings about the morality of abortion. In the same 2013 WSJ/NBC report, almost seven in ten Americans surveyed said that there were some circumstances when abortion should not be allowed. In another 2013 survey from Rasmussen Reports, 51 percent of voting adults said they believed abortion to be morally wrong most of

"At the end of the day, Americans are committed to the availability of abortion, and conflicted about its morality."[16]

— Robert P. Jones, chief executive of the Public Religion Research Institute.

the time. "At the end of the day, Americans are committed to the availability of abortion, and conflicted about its morality," says Robert P. Jones. "I would call it a stable tension."[16]

When Does Life Begin?

Central to the morality debate is the issue of when life begins. How a person views this issue, in many cases, shapes one's perspective on abortion. Depending on a person's beliefs about the beginning of life, abortion can be considered either a simple medical procedure or the murder of an innocent life. Pro-life advocates believe that life begins at the moment of conception. In their view, abortion is the murder of an unborn child.

On the other side, pro-choice abortion rights advocates argue that life begins at a later point. Some believe that life begins when a fetus becomes viable, while others believe life begins at birth. Under the view that life does not begin at conception, abortion is a moral choice. "Abortion is not a question of Christians vs. non-Christians; it is not a question of Democrats vs. Republicans and it is not a question of men vs. women. Abortion is a question of life. It is a question of when our children are alive and what we do to protect their lives,"[17] writes columnist Calum Hayes for the Annenberg School for Communication and Journalism.

"Abortion is killing a baby, it's murder. It's something that should not be legal. I want to stand up against it and hope we can make a change."[18]

— Marissa Tackett, antiabortion supporter.

Life Begins at Conception

In 2013 Mike and Marissa Tackett of Goodyear, Arizona, attended an antiabortion rally at a Phoenix abortion clinic. Along with other attendees, they lined the road in front of the clinic, protesting the abortions performed there. Like many Americans the Tacketts believe that abortion is morally wrong. "Abortion is killing a baby, it's murder," says Marissa. "It's something that should not be legal. I want to stand up against it and hope we can make a change."[18]

People who share the view of the Tacketts believe that life begins at conception, when a sperm fertilizes an egg and forms a one-celled zygote. According to the National Right to Life website, "the life of a baby begins long before he or she is born. A new individual human being begins at fertilization, when the sperm and ovum meet to form a single cell."[19]

In this view, from the moment of fertilization the fetus has the same rights as any other person and therefore abortion is the same as killing a person and thus an immoral act. During a 2013 address to the National Right to Life convention, Texas governor Rick Perry expressed this perspective when he said, "In the four decades since *Roe v. Wade*, more than 50 million children have lost their chance at life. Even in Texas, where the unborn are already more protected than in most places, nearly 80,000 unborn children are lost to abortion each year. Every time I hear that statistic, it breaks my heart; nearly 80,000 lives lost before taking their first breath."[20]

In hope of giving this position the force of law, in 2011 pro-life activists in Mississippi pushed Initiative 26, an amendment to the state constitution that would have defined life to include every human being from the moment of fertilization. Voters rejected the initiative but pro-life advocates remain steadfast in their support of this view. Joseph DeCook, executive director of the American Association of Pro-life Obstetricians and Gynecologists and a supporter of Initiative 26, says that an embryo is a living human being from the moment of fertilization. "There's no question at all when human life begins," says DeCook. "When the two sets of chromosomes get together, you have a complete individual. It's the same as you and I but less developed."[21]

> "There's no question at all when human life begins. When the two sets of chromosomes get together, you have a complete individual. It's the same as you and I but less developed."[21]
>
> — Joseph DeCook, executive director of the American Association of Pro-life Obstetricians and Gynecologists.

Conception Is a Biological Beginning

For others, conception marks the biological beginning of life and a potential for the growth of a human being. At this early stage, in this view, a whole person does not yet exist—nor will it for a period of time. Fertilization is just the first stage in the reproductive process—and it does not always lead to pregnancy. In this view, "A fertilized egg has to continue to grow, attach itself to a woman's uterine wall and gestate for nine months before it is born,

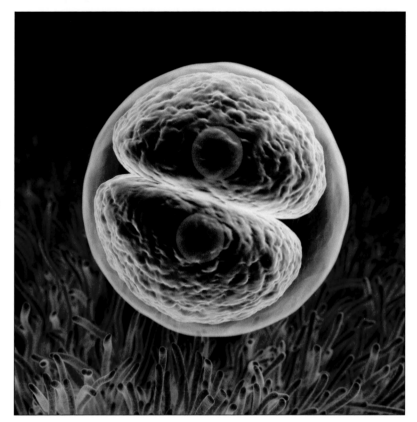

Some Americans believe that life begins at conception, when a sperm fertilizes an egg and forms a zygote (pictured here at twenty-four to thirty-six hours of development). From this point on, in this view, the growing life has all of the rights of any other human being.

and there are many potential missteps (that can happen) along the way," says Sean Tipton, spokesman for the American Society for Reproductive Medicine, which represents fertility specialists in the United States and countries worldwide. Tipton explains that although an egg and sperm may meet, it can take several more days for a fertilized egg to implant in the woman's uterus, the start of pregnancy. Many fertilized eggs do not implant successfully, and pregnancy never begins. "There are lots of fertilized eggs that never become human beings,"[22] Tipton says.

The issue of when life begins is rooted in religious beliefs and moral values, abortion rights advocates say, and therefore should not determine the legality of abortion. In this view, the decision to have or not to have an abortion properly belongs with the woman, not with a standard influenced by one religion or another. As the Wisconsin chapter of NARAL, an abortion rights organization, states, "There are many different moral and religious views on that question. In a country that embraces and is tolerant of a variety of religious views, it is important to avoid adopting one religious view over another. That is why every woman should have the right to examine her own religious, spiritual and ethical beliefs in deciding what is best for her and her family, rather than allowing the government to impose one view on all Americans."[23]

In addition, abortion rights advocates contend that just because a fetus is alive from a biological sense, it does not immediately have a legal right to life. Organisms such as plants and animals are alive, but it is generally accepted that their rights should be secondary to those of human beings. According NARAL, "Eggs and sperm are alive; so are bacteria and all plants and animals. Of course, embryos and fetuses are alive. That doesn't mean, though, that abortion should be illegal or that it constitutes murder. The Supreme Court has said . . . that legal personhood begins with birth. The *Roe v. Wade* decision allowed states to ban abortion after the fetus could live on its own, after viability, with certain exceptions, but it did not say that a viable fetus was a legal person."[24]

Fetal Viability

Establishing the point of fetal viability, or when a fetus can survive outside the womb, is harder than it sounds. The human fetus develops over a forty-week period. This period is commonly divided into three trimesters. In the first trimester, a single-cell zygote forms. The zygote grows through cell division, attaches to the woman's uterus, and forms an embryo. Around the fifth week of development the embryo's brain begins to form and its heart begins to beat. At the beginning of the second trimester, at around thirteen weeks, the embryo is called a fetus. It continues to grow, and at around the sixteenth to twentieth week the woman can feel fetal movement. At the beginning of the third trimester, at twenty-seven weeks, the fetus has developed enough that it could potentially survive outside the womb, a point called viability.

In its *Roe v. Wade* decision, the Supreme Court ruled that the

"Every woman should have the right to examine her own religious, spiritual and ethical beliefs in deciding what is best for her and her family, rather than allowing the government to impose one view on all Americans."[23]

— NARAL Pro Choice Wisconsin.

Career Versus Conscience

Health professionals who have moral objections to abortion have, at times, faced a dilemma over whether to take part in performing abortions. In 2009 when nurse Cathy DeCarlo arrived at Mt. Sinai Hospital in New York for her shift, she was ordered to assist in an abortion of a twenty-two-week-old fetus. DeCarlo is a Catholic and morally objects to abortion. When she was hired, she told the hospital that she was unwilling to perform abortions—and the hospital agreed that she would not have to assist in any abortions. In line with this agreement, DeCarlo asked her supervisor to find a replacement nurse for the procedure. The head nurse informed DeCarlo that she would have to assist with the abortion or face disciplinary action, putting her career in jeopardy. Afraid of losing her job, DeCarlo assisted in the abortion. Afterward, she experienced nightmares and insomnia over her role in the procedure. "I couldn't believe that this could happen. I felt violated and betrayed," she said.

Congress and various medical professional organizations have sought ways to address this type of conflict. The worry, from the abortion rights perspective, is that patients might be unable to obtain the care they need if health professionals can opt out of providing certain services. In some instances, health providers have even refused to refer patients to others who will perform those services. Says Adam Sonfield at the pro-choice Guttmacher Institute, "There are some lines you can't cross. You can't deny information. You can't deny care in an emergency, and if you refuse care, you must make sure the patient isn't abandoned."

Quoted in Eric Schulzke, "Pro-Life Health Professionals in Conflict Between Conscience and Career," *Deseret News*, March 17, 2012. www.deseretnews.com.

interests of the fetus could not be placed above the interests of the mother until the fetus was viable outside the womb. The court accepted the prevailing medical opinion of the time, which was that viability occurs at around twenty-eight weeks. Using a trimester analysis, the court's ruling permitted no government regulation of abortion during the first trimester of pregnancy, permitted limited regulation in the second trimester to protect a woman's health and safety, and granted state governments the right to ban abortions during the third trimester. In a later ruling the court rejected the trimester framework while affirming the central holding that a woman has a right to obtain an abortion until viability—usually at around twenty-four to twenty-eight weeks.

Does a Fetus Feel Pain?

In 2010 Nebraska added a new twist to the debate over the morality of abortion. By an overwhelming majority the state legislature passed the first ever bill banning abortions after twenty weeks gestation, based on the idea that a fetus can feel pain at that stage of development. "Determining when the fetus can feel and suffer from such pain does seem important. After all, many moral arguments are based on the capacity of beings to experience pain. For example, stock arguments in the moral debate over the treatment of animals rest on the fact that many of the ways we treat animals (such as how we raise them as food) causes them pain and suffering. If the pain and suffering of animals matters morally, then it would certainly seem that the pain and suffering of fetuses would also matter morally,"[25] says Michael LaBossiere, professor of philosophy at Florida A&M University.

Nebraska's governor quickly signed the bill into law. "The Nebraska Legislature took a bold step today which should ratchet up the abortion debate across America," said Julie Schmit-Albin, executive director of Nebraska Right to Life, in a statement in 2010. "LB 1103 creates a case of first impression for the courts to acknowledge the capability to feel pain as a compelling state interest to protect those unborn babies from an excruciatingly painful death."[26] Since 2010 ten states have followed Nebraska's lead, enacting similar laws.

Supporters of these laws say that by twenty weeks and possibly earlier a fetus has developed pain receptors and can therefore feel pain. The NRLC cites several sources that support this claim, including *Gregory's Pediatric Anesthesia* published by the University of California at San Francisco, which states that sensory receptors that send signals that cause the perception of pain are present between ten and seventeen weeks in a developing fetus. "At 20 weeks, the fetal brain has the full complement of brain cells present in adulthood, ready and waiting to receive pain signals from the body, and their electrical activity can be recorded by standard electroencephalography (EEG),"[27] says Paul Ranalli, a neurologist at the University of Toronto.

Challenges to Fetal Pain Laws

Critics of laws that restrict abortion based on what a fetus can feel and when argue that scientific research does not support these claims. After the passage of the Nebraska law, the American College of Obstetricians and Gynecologists, a nonprofit organization of women's health care physicians, issued a statement saying there is "no legitimate scientific information that supports the statement that a fetus experiences pain."[28] The consensus in the medical community is that a fetus may exhibit reflexes before viability, but its nervous system does not develop enough to feel pain until sometime during the third trimester.

In a study published in the journal *Current Biology* in 2011, scientists from London's University College Hospital looked at the brain activity of forty-six babies, twenty-one of whom were born prematurely. Scientists tracked electrical activity in their brains while blood samples were collected using a heel lance. In the premature babies' brains, researchers saw a general burst of electrical activity, similar to that experienced in response to touch. In contrast, researchers found that those born after thirty-five to thirty-seven weeks experienced a response in a specific area of the brain, which suggested they felt pain. The researchers concluded that the brain's neural activity gradually changed from an immature state to a more mature state at around thirty-five weeks of development. "Premature babies who are younger than 35 weeks have similar

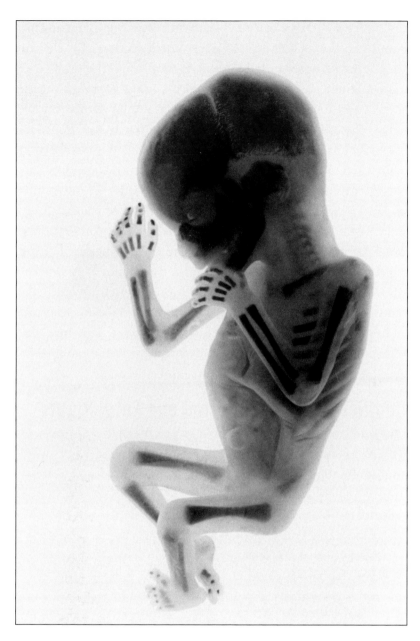

One point of contention in the abortion debate is at what point a fetus is viable outside the womb. With medical advances, the point of viability is now considered to be about twenty-four to twenty-eight weeks. A twenty-four-week-old fetus is pictured.

brain responses when they experience touch or pain. After this time there is a gradual change, rather than a sudden shift, when the brain starts to process the two types of stimuli in a distinct manner,"[29] says Rebeccah Slater of the University College London's Department of Neuroscience, Physiology and Pharmacology.

Challenges to these laws are now making their way through

the courts. In 2013 a federal court struck down an Idaho law that banned abortions after twenty weeks based on the belief that the fetus could feel pain at that stage of development. The ruling cited the Supreme Court's *Roe v. Wade* and *Planned Parenthood v. Casey* rulings and reiterated that a woman has a right to an abortion before the point of viability. The decision stated that the Idaho law placed an undue burden on the woman's right to an abortion. "For 40 years, the Supreme Court has consistently held that women's right to make their own decisions about whether to continue or end a pregnancy is guaranteed by the U.S. Constitution," says Julie Rikelman, litigation director for the Center for Reproductive Rights, in a statement that applauded the court's decision. "Today's ruling has overturned a legislative assault by politicians who seek to interfere with that decision and deny women this fundamental right."[30] In its decision the court did not specifically address the issue of whether a fetus can feel pain. That issue may surface in a future ruling. In the meantime, this and other moral issues surrounding abortion continue to be debated.

Conflict Between Maternal and Fetal Rights

One of the ongoing moral quandaries pits the rights of a pregnant woman against the rights of the fetus. If the interests of the woman and the fetus are in conflict, which one should take priority? This issue divides along the usual lines, with some arguing that the rights of the woman should always take precedence over the rights of the fetus and others arguing that the rights of the fetus should override any other considerations.

Even if a fetus is considered to be a human being, some abortion rights advocates believe that the woman's rights should always take priority over the rights of the fetus. "Here's the complicated reality in which we live: All life is not equal. . . . Yet a fetus can be a human life without having the same rights as the woman in whose body it resides. She's the boss. Her life and what is right for her circumstances and her health should automatically trump the rights of the non-autonomous entity inside of her. Always,"[31] writes Mary Elizabeth Williams, a journalist who identifies herself as pro-choice.

For some abortion opponents, however, there are no circumstances that make abortion a moral choice. For those who take this position, the unborn child's right to live always supersedes any and all rights of the woman. While the pro-life National Right to Life Committee has made a statement that abortions should be allowed in rare cases to save a woman's life, a stricter view is held by another antiabortion group, the American Life League. This group says that "there is never a situation in the law or in the ethical practice of medicine where a preborn child's life need be intentionally destroyed. . . . A physician must do everything possible to save the lives of both of his patients, mother and child. He must never intend the death of either."[32]

Balancing Rights

For many Americans, the balance of rights falls somewhere in the middle of the two extremes. Most Americans believe that maternal rights supersede the fetus in certain situations. If a woman becomes pregnant as a result of rape or incest, or if the pregnancy puts her life or health in danger, they believe that it is morally acceptable to place the rights of the woman above those of the fetus. In a 2013 poll conducted by the *Wall Street Journal* and NBC almost 90 percent of respondents said they thought abortion was acceptable in circumstances such as rape, incest, and to save a woman's life.

Many people believe that maternal rights should be given priority over those of a fetus when abortion is necessary to save the woman's life. Life-threatening conditions during pregnancy include severe infections, heart failure, and severe cases of preeclampsia, a sudden rise in blood pressure that puts the woman at risk for a stroke. "There are certain cases where ending the pregnancy is the only option, cases where it would be putting the mother's life at risk to continue the pregnancy,"[33] says Erika Levi, an obstetrician and gynecologist at the University of North Carolina, Chapel Hill.

In 2004 forty-four-year-old Cecily Kellogg of Philadelphia, Pennsylvania, was nearly six months pregnant with twin boys. She

> "There are certain cases where ending the pregnancy is the only option, cases where it would be putting the mother's life at risk to continue the pregnancy."[33]
>
> — Erika Levi, an obstetrician and gynecologist at the University of North Carolina, Chapel Hill.

Violence in the Name of Morality

Since abortion became legal in the United States in 1973, some antiabortion extremists have resorted to violence against abortion clinics and providers. The first reported clinic arson took place in 1976, and several clinic bombings occurred in 1978. Other extremists used chemicals to block women's access to clinics and sent anthrax threat letters to scare clinic employees. In 1993 David Gunn, who ran an abortion clinic in Pensacola, Florida, was shot to death outside the clinic by an antiabortion extremist. According to the National Abortion Federation, eight abortion providers have been killed since 1977, and there have been seventeen incidents of attempted murder. In addition, there have been more than six thousand incidents of violence against abortion providers and clinics, including bombings, vandalism, trespassing, and death threats.

Many antiabortion advocates have condemned the actions of these extremists. After the 2009 murder of George Tiller, a Kansas abortion provider, the National Right to Life Committee issued a statement saying that "We always have and will continue to oppose any form of violence to fight the violence of abortion."

Not all have let the antiabortion movement off the hook, however. Writer Frank Schaeffer, once an outspoken critic of abortion rights, believes the tone and texture of comments by pro-life groups are partly to blame for the violence. "I—and the people I worked with in the religious right, the Republican Party, the pro-life movement and the Roman Catholic Church, all contributed to this killing by our foolish and incendiary words," Schaeffer wrote shortly after Tiller's murder.

NRLC, "National Right to Life Condemns Killing of Dr. George Tiller," press release, May 31, 2009. www.nrlc.org.

Frank Schaeffer, "How I (and Other Pro-Life Leaders) Contributed to Dr. Tiller's Murder," *Huffington Post*, June 1, 2009. www.huffingtonpost.com.

developed severe preeclampsia, a condition resulting in danger-ously high blood pressure and putting her at risk for a stroke. Af-ter one fetus died and Kellogg's own life was in jeopardy, doctors advised her to have an abortion to save her life. "My liver had shut down, my kidneys had shut down and they were expecting me to start seizing at any minute," she says. "I fought it. But they told me I would die—that it was either me and my son or just my son."[34] Kellogg chose to have the abortion.

The Murder of George Tiller

The moral conflict over abortion has, on occasion, taken some extreme turns. On May 31, 2009, fifty-one-year-old antiabortion activist Scott Roeder of Kansas City, Missouri, shot and killed sixty-seven-year-old George Tiller as he stood in the foyer of his Wichita, Kansas, church. One of the few doctors in the country who performed abortions late in a woman's pregnancy, Tiller and his clinic had been the target of violence before. In 1986 an anti-abortion activist bombed Tiller's clinic. In 1993 another antiabor-tion extremist shot Tiller in both arms.

After the fatal shooting, police arrested Roeder and charged him with first-degree murder. In November 2009 Roeder spoke to reporters from jail and publicly confessed to the killing. Roeder said that he was morally justified in shooting Tiller because he was defending the lives of unborn children. "Because of the fact pre-born children's lives were in imminent danger this was the action I chose. . . . I want to make sure that the focus is, of course, obvi-ously on the preborn children and the necessity to defend them," Roeder said. "Defending innocent life—that is what prompted me. It is pretty simple."[35] In 2010 Roeder was found guilty of first-degree murder and two counts of aggravated assault. He was sentenced to life imprisonment without any chance for parole be-fore fifty years.

Several antiabortion activists condemned the murder. Troy Newman, the president of Operation Rescue, an antiabortion group based in Wichita, said he had always attempted to use non-violent methods to protest Tiller's activities. "Operation Rescue has worked tirelessly on peaceful, nonviolent measures to bring him to justice through the legal system, the legislative system," says Newman. "We are pro-life, and this act was antithetical to what we believe."[36]

Conflicted Views

The morality of abortion is a complex and nuanced topic. Abortion puts the rights of the woman and the fetus in direct conflict with one another. A 2013 Pew Research Center poll illustrates the deeply conflicted views Americans hold on abortion, with the majority in support of upholding *Roe v. Wade* (63 percent). Even though they supported keeping abortion legal, the same respondents were morally conflicted about the procedure, with nearly half (47 percent) saying that abortion is morally wrong and only 13 percent saying it is morally acceptable. "On the issue of abortion, many Americans hold complex views and fluid identities," says Daniel Cox, research director at the Public Religion Research Institute. "For some time now, Americans have held a stable tension between two views: majorities both say that abortion is morally wrong and say that it should be legal in all or most cases. The binary 'pro-life' and 'pro-choice' labels don't reflect this complexity."[37]

Facts

- Of women who have had an abortion in the United States, 43 percent identify themselves as Protestant, 27 percent as Catholic, and 13 percent as born-again or Evangelical Christians, reports the Orlando Women's Center.

- Women are more likely than men to be pro-choice and are less likely to consider abortion morally wrong in most cases, according to Rasmussen Reports.

- Voters with children in the home are more likely to be pro-life and to consider abortion morally wrong most of the time, compared to those without children living with them.

- A 2013 Gallup poll found that 26 percent of Americans say abortion should be legal under any circumstances, 20 percent say it should be illegal in all circumstances, and 52 percent opt for something in between.

- In 1973 Congress passed the Church amendments, named after Senator Frank Church of Idaho, to protect health care professionals from being forced to assist in abortions in the aftermath of *Roe v. Wade*.

Should States Have the Right to Place Limits on Abortion?

In the *Roe v. Wade* ruling the Supreme Court noted that states have an interest in safeguarding health, maintaining medical standards, and protecting potential life, opening the door for state regulation of abortion. In the years since that ruling, many states have used that language as justification for the adoption of laws that regulate abortion. While some claim that these regulations are necessary to ensure the health and safety of women, others contend that many of these laws are aimed at impeding access to abortion.

Moving the Fight to the States

Antiabortion groups have made several unsuccessful attempts to overturn the abortion rights granted in the *Roe* decision. In 1976 the court overturned a Missouri law in *Planned Parenthood v. Danforth* that required a woman to obtain her husband's consent for an abortion. In 1990 the court struck down a Minnesota law in *Hodgson v. Minnesota* that required minors to notify both parents before having an abortion. In the 1992 *Planned Parenthood of Southeastern Pennsylvania v. Casey* decision the court upheld several Pennsylvania abortion regulations but also upheld Roe's central principle that women have a constitutional right to abortion. Other cases challenging abortion restrictions have had similar outcomes. "I think there's a lot of frustration in the pro-life movement," says Paul B. Linton, a constitutional lawyer in Illinois who was formerly general counsel of Americans United for Life. "Forty years after *Roe v. Wade* was decided, it's still the law of the land."[38]

As a result, abortion opponents have taken their fight to state legislatures, where they have had more success. In 2011 twenty-four states passed a total of ninety-two abortion restrictions. In 2012 nineteen states enacted forty-three provisions to restrict access to abortion services.

Some state laws regulate the circumstances under which a woman can have an abortion. The law may require a woman to have an ultrasound or wait for a mandatory period, usually twenty-four hours, before having an abortion. Other regulations require that women receive counseling about the risks of the procedure. Some states require counseling that includes information about a potential link between abortion and breast cancer, fetal pain, or the long-term mental health consequences of abortion. If the woman seeking an abortion is a minor, some states require that she obtain parental consent or notify a parent about her intention to have an abortion. Other state laws limit or ban health insurance coverage of the costs of abortion.

In many cases these requirements place a burden on women seeking abortion, particularly on low-income and rural women. Low-income women may not be able to pay for an abortion if the procedure is not covered by insurance. Some women may have difficulty taking time away from work, finding childcare, and traveling to a clinic provider—first, for the mandatory counseling, and again after the mandatory waiting period—in order to obtain an abortion. Minors in states with parental consent or notification laws are forced to tell parents about an unplanned pregnancy if they do not have the resources to travel to another state without a consent law.

Other state restrictions target abortion providers and clinics, making it harder for them to operate. As of 2013 nine states had laws that require abortion doctors to have hospital admitting privileges with a local hospital, allowing them to practice in that hospital. Some hospitals, especially religious-based and publicly funded hospitals, are reluctant to grant privileges to abortion providers. When Mississippi passed a bill in 2012 requiring abortion provid-

Increasing Access

While several states have passed legislation to restrict access and regulate abortion, a few states have proposed legislation with the opposite intention—to increase women's access and coverage for abortion. In 2013, California passed legislation that allows licensed nurse practitioners, physician assistants, and nurse midwives to perform aspiration abortions during a woman's first trimester. Oregon, Montana, Vermont, and New Hampshire already have similar legislation in place.

In Washington State, lawmakers are attempting to pass legislation that would make the state the first with explicit requirements for insurers to cover the cost of abortion. If passed, the mandate would apply to all health plans that are sold through the state's insurance exchange created by the Affordable Care Act, signed into law in 2010. Laurie Jinkins, a Washington State representative from Tacoma, says that the trend toward more abortion restrictions in other states has energized abortion rights groups in Washington. "There's a huge attack on women's reproductive health. Everything from our access to simple birth control to the right to choose to have an abortion if that's what you decide to do. . . . It does make it more clear why in states like Washington, where we've had a 40-year history of protecting women's rights, why we need to make sure that we keep on doing it," says Jinkins.

Quoted in Ariel Edwards-Levy, "Abortion Laws Proposed in Some States Would Buck National Trend, Expand Access," *Huffington Post*, April 24, 2012. www.huffingtonpost.com.

ers to have admitting privileges, many hospitals refused, which caused most of the state's clinics to close. Other laws require abortion clinics to undergo significant and costly renovations to become ambulatory surgical centers, a type of mini-hospital. In Alabama, House Bill 57 reclassifies abortion providers as clinics that provide outpatient surgery. Under this classification the clinics are required to meet certain fire codes, submit architectural drawings and sprinkler plans within 180 days, and receive a certificate of compliance within a year. For many clinics the regulations require an extensive and costly redesign and modification of the facility.

Still other state restrictions have banned procedures prior to fetal viability, in direct conflict with the Supreme Court's *Roe v. Wade* ruling. States such as Indiana, Kansas, and Louisiana have banned abortion after twenty weeks.

North Dakota's Tough Abortion Restrictions

This fight at the state level is exactly what happened in North Dakota in 2013, when state legislators approved the country's toughest abortion restrictions, signing into law a measure that would ban nearly all abortions. The law forbids abortion once a fetal heartbeat is detectable, which can be as early as six weeks into a pregnancy. Another North Dakota law bans abortion for gender selection or genetic defects, the first such law in the country. A third state law requires abortion doctors to have admitting privileges at a local hospital, which could close clinics if doctors were denied access by local hospitals. "This is just a great day for babies in North Dakota," says Bette Grande, a North Dakota State representative and primary sponsor of the heartbeat bill. "The state has a compelling duty to find what is the potential life of a fetus. What is more compelling and proof of life than a heartbeat? It meets the criteria of *Roe v. Wade*."[39]

Abortion rights advocates protested that the North Dakota laws were a direct and unconstitutional assault on women's right to abortion. "North Dakota has set a new standard for extreme hostility toward the rights and health of women, the U.S. Constitution, and 40 years of Supreme Court precedent. We will not allow this frontal assault on fundamental reproductive rights to go

Members of an abortion rights group rally in Fargo, North Dakota, in 2013 to protest a new state law that bans nearly all abortions.

unchallenged," says Nancy Northup, president and CEO of the Center for Reproductive Rights. Northup believes that North Dakota's restrictive state laws will cause more harm to women in the state. "We don't need to guess about the brutal harm this criminalization of abortion will cause. We know from the United States' own shameful history prior to *Roe v. Wade* and from examples around the world that women desperate to end a pregnancy will find ways to do so whether it is safe and legal or not—and some will suffer and die as a result,"[40] she says.

Protecting Women's Health

Proponents of state abortion laws argue that the regulations protect women's health by making sure that abortions are provided in a safe and controlled environment. These laws may require clinics to meet certain facility safety standards, follow specific procedures, or use doctors with admitting privileges at local hospitals. If a clinic or provider does not meet state standards, it can be shut down.

In 2013 North Carolina state inspectors shut down the Baker Clinic for Women in Durham, after a routine inspection of the facility found that it had failed to follow standard quality control procedures for blood banking. "This is exactly the type of substandard 'medical' care threatening women's health that we intended to fight,"[41] says North Carolina State senator Phil Berger.

Yet some people are concerned that states are overstepping their bounds in enacting abortion restrictions. As North Carolina lawmakers considered legislation in 2013 that would require abortion clinics to meet the same standards as ambulatory surgical centers, North Carolina's governor Pat McCrory expressed his concern over the proposed legislation. He said that there was a fine line between safety measures to protect health and restrictions to limit abortion rights and that those goals should not be confused. When asked whether he viewed the abortion bill as primarily dealing with women's safety or restricting access, McCrory said that he thought more discussion was needed. "I think parts of the bill, personally, deal with safety and help protect these women, as has been seen in Durham. But I also see that there are parts of the bill that clearly cross that line that could add further restrictions to that access."[42]

Increasing Obstacles to Limit Abortion

Abortion rights advocates argue that state regulations passed under the guise of protecting women's health are a flimsy excuse to impose restrictions that increase costs and obstacles for abortion providers and the women who seek these procedures. "This has nothing to do with patient safety," says obstetrician/gynecologist John Baker. "Legislators around the country are trying to legislate abortion out of existence. They can only go so far, so they go as far as they can."[43]

Abortion rights activists call these state laws "TRAP" laws—targeted regulation of abortion providers. According to the National Abortion Federation, TRAP bills single out abortion providers for medically unnecessary regulations that can force clinics to remodel extensively or to hire additional staff. According to a 2013 *Huffington Post* nationwide survey of state health departments, abortion clinics, and local abortion advocacy groups, at least fifty-four abortion providers in twenty-seven states shut down or stopped providing abortion services between 2010 and 2013. Several other clinics remain open only because judges have temporarily blocked state regulations that would close the clinics. In Arizona, lawmakers passed legislation requiring abortion clinics to become ambulatory surgical centers and abortion doctors to have admitting privileges at a local hospital. Between 2010 and 2013 Arizona's abortion providers dropped from eighteen to six. "At the end of the day, all of it is about a strategy to chip away and undermine access to the right to an abortion," says Louise Melling, a deputy legal director of the ACLU. "Each restriction is kind of a brick, and you keep adding one brick year after year—how long before the wall becomes so high women can't access abortion in those states?"[44]

Abortion rights groups have responded to state regulations that restrict abortion by filing legal challenges. They claim that the state regulations are a blatant attempt to circumvent *Roe v. Wade* and deprive women of their constitutional right to have an abortion. These groups have called for any state law that violates this right to be struck down as unconstitutional. In Wisconsin, the ACLU, Planned Parenthood Federation of America, and other abortion rights groups filed a complaint in 2013 against a restriction that required doctors who performed abortions to have admitting privileges at local hospitals. The abortion rights groups argued that this restriction unconstitutionally limited a woman's access to abortion by restricting the number of doctors who could legally perform the procedure. In response, US district judge William Conley issued a temporary restraining order blocking the Wisconsin abortion law. In his ruling Judge Conley says that "there is a troubling lack of justification for the hospital admitting privileges requirement." He notes that the US Supreme Court has ruled that states must prove that restrictions on abortion rights are reasonably aimed at preserving the mother's health. "Moreover, the record to date strongly supports a finding that no medical purpose is served by this requirement,"[45] he says.

"*Each restriction is kind of a brick, and you keep adding one brick year after year—how long before the wall becomes so high women can't access abortion in those states?*"[44]

— Louise Melling, a deputy legal director of the American Civil Liberties Union (ACLU).

Challenging *Roe v. Wade*

Some antiabortion groups view efforts to restrict abortion at the state level as part of a larger plan to get abortion once again before the Supreme Court. The current makeup of the court is more conservative than in past years. These groups hope that the court as it is currently constituted would overturn *Roe v. Wade* if a challenge came before it. Several states have passed new laws that may trig-

Traveling Greater Distances

Although abortion is legal in the United States, restrictions in some states make it difficult for women to find a qualified provider. According to a 2013 study by the Guttmacher Institute, the average American woman travels thirty miles for abortion services. In addition, 74 percent of women who live in rural areas travel more than fifty miles for abortion care, while one-third of rural women travel more than one hundred miles.

In some states women are forced to travel even farther for abortion services. In Wisconsin, women living in the Green Bay area have to make a 250-mile trip for an abortion, after the only Green Bay area clinic stopped providing abortion services in 2013. In North Dakota and Mississippi, there is only one abortion clinic open to serve the entire state. "Many women travel substantial distances to access abortion services. This can present a barrier, particularly for poor and low-income women, who make up the majority of women seeking abortions, and for women in rural areas," says Rachel Jones, the Guttmacher study's lead author. "For women in states with mandatory counseling and waiting periods, the barrier is even greater, and one [that] some women may not be able to overcome."

Quoted in Guttmacher Institute, "One-Third of U.S. Women Seeking Abortions Travel More than 25 Miles to Access Services," July 26, 2013. http://www.guttmacher.org.

ger a constitutional challenge to *Roe*. North Dakota banned most abortions after six weeks, Arkansas banned them at twelve weeks, and Alabama implemented new safety standards for abortion clinics that may force several to close. Any of these state laws may be challenged and eventually heard by the Supreme Court.

Americans United for Life (AUL) is an organization that advises conservative politicians who are trying to limit state abortion rights. In the first six months of 2013 seventeen states enacted forty-five new restrictions on abortion, and many of them were assisted by AUL. "In order for the court to actually reconsider *Roe*, it has to have an active case before it. So we work with legislators to pass laws that will essentially spark the right kind of court challenge and give [the court] the opportunity to reconsider the question,"[46] says Daniel McConchie, AUL's vice president for government affairs.

To increase the number of laws that challenge *Roe*, AUL publishes a seven-hundred-page antiabortion guide called *Defending Life*. The guide has forty-eight pre-written bills that politicians can copy and introduce in their states. "Our model legislation is specifically tailored to confront the current trends in Big Abortion's overreach," says Charmaine Yoest, AUL president. "*Defending Life* is a game changer, constitutionally sound legislation that can rewrite the laws of the nation to protect life."[47]

North Dakota's tough abortion restrictions, signed into law in 2013, are an example of state legislation created with the help of AUL. Grande credits AUL with helping her get the bill passed. AUL gave Grande a cut-and-paste model bill, statistics, and talking points. AUL also provided Grande with the legal justification for the legislation and the arguments she used to convince her fellow representatives to support the law. They provided "good, factual information regarding abnormalities and the discrimination that occurs inside the womb," she says. "My colleagues didn't need a whole lot of persuasion after that."[48] AUL leaders hope that North Dakota's success in passing the tough

"*In order for the court to actually reconsider Roe, it has to have an active case before it. So we work with legislators to pass laws that will essentially spark the right kind of court challenge and give [the court] the opportunity to reconsider the question.*"[46]

— Daniel McConchie, Americans United for Life's vice president for government affairs.

A single protester expresses her views on abortion in Dallas, Texas, in 2013. Texas is among the states that has adopted new restrictive abortion laws.

restrictions will encourage other states to pass similar legislation.

The North Dakota fetal-heartbeat laws and others like them may one day be challenged in the Supreme Court. Opponents of these fetal-heartbeat laws say that they violate *Roe v. Wade*. In previous challenges however, the Supreme Court has never considered the heartbeat restriction. North Dakota's law and other similar state laws may be declared unconstitutional if challenged in federal court. "Although the likelihood of this measure surviving a court challenge remains in question, this bill is nevertheless a legitimate attempt by a state legislature to discover the boundaries of *Roe v. Wade*,"[49] said Governor Jack Dalrymple of North Dakota in a statement after signing the regulations into law.

Fighting Back in the Courts

Abortion rights supporters have challenged many of the new state laws—and have had varying degrees of success. In 2013 a federal appellate panel struck down Arizona's ban on abortions prior to viability. Passed in 2012, the law made it illegal for abortions to be performed twenty weeks after a woman's last menstrual period or at about eighteen weeks gestation. This included cases where the fetus had no chance of survival after birth. The ACLU and other abortion rights groups challenged the law in federal court on behalf of three doctors and their patients. "Politicians do not have the right to interfere in serious and personal decisions that should only be made by a woman with the help of her family and her doctor,"[50] says Talcott Camp, deputy director of the ACLU's reproductive freedom project.

The case was heard by a panel of three federal judges. They ruled that the viability of a fetus should be determined by a woman's doctor, not by law. "While the state may regulate the model and manner of abortion prior to fetal viability, it may not proscribe a woman from electing abortion, nor may it impose an undue burden on her choice through regulation,"[51] writes Judge Marsha S. Berzon, author of the court's opinion. The decision applies to Arizona and eight other western states under the federal panel's jurisdiction.

In other cases, however, state laws that place restrictions or conditions on abortions have had more success withstanding legal challenges. In 2013 the Illinois Supreme Court ruled that the 1995 Parental Notice of Abortion Act that requires parental notification is constitutional. The law requires doctors to inform the parents of girls aged seventeen and under that their daughter wants to have an abortion. Justice Anne Burke writes in the court's majority opinion: "We find that, while a minor clearly has an expectation of privacy in her medical information, which includes the fact of her pregnancy, the intrusion on the minor's privacy occasioned by the Act is not unreasonable."[52]

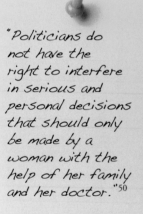

"Politicians do not have the right to interfere in serious and personal decisions that should only be made by a woman with the help of her family and her doctor."[50]

— Talcott Camp, deputy director of the ACLU's reproductive freedom project.

Burke further explains that the state has an interest in making sure a minor is mature enough and has enough information to make an educated decision about whether or not to have an abortion. The majority opinion also cites several US Supreme Court cases that upheld state laws that require parental notification for abortion. "We conclude, therefore, that our Parental Notice Act furthers a 'constitutionally permissible end' by encouraging an unmarried, pregnant minor to seek the help and advice of a parent or other adult family member in making the very important decision whether or not to bear a child,"[53] says Burke.

The Divided States

In the years since the Supreme Court issued the *Roe v. Wade* ruling and legalized abortion, individual states have interpreted the law and their role in regulating abortion in different ways. Some state legislatures have passed strict limits on abortion, while others debate strong legal protections for the procedure. Because of this divide, access to abortion varies widely from state to state. "A state may have anywhere from zero to one or two laws around restricting access, all the way up to a dozen or more," says Elizabeth Nash, who manages state issues for the Guttmacher Institute. "Your access to reproductive healthcare depends greatly on where you live."[54]

> *"Your access to reproductive healthcare depends greatly on where you live."*[54]
>
> — Elizabeth Nash of the Guttmacher Institute, a nonprofit organization that monitors and supports abortion rights.

Facts

- According to a 2013 Rasmussen Reports survey, 23 percent of Americans believe it is too hard to get an abortion in the United States; thirty-nine percent think it is too easy to get an abortion; and 25 percent feel the level of difficulty is about right.

- According to a 2013 Rasmussen Reports survey, 45 percent of respondents think there should be a mandatory waiting period before a woman is allowed to get an abortion, while 42 percent disagree.

- According to the Guttmacher Institute, thirty-five states require women to receive counseling before an abortion is performed.

- Forty-six states allow some health care providers to refuse to provide abortion services, according to the Guttmacher Institute.

- According to the National Abortion Federation, 61 percent of minors told one or both parents about their abortion, even without state laws requiring notification.

Should Late-Term Abortions Be Banned?

K ermit Gosnell, a seventy-two-year-old doctor who operated a Philadelphia abortion clinic, was convicted in May 2013 of three counts of first-degree murder after cutting the spines of babies in late-term abortions gone wrong. Gosnell was also found guilty of twenty-four counts of performing an abortion beyond twenty-four weeks, the point at which abortions are banned in Pennsylvania. During Gosnell's trial prosecutors called his clinic a house of horrors and presented graphic evidence about unsanitary and unsafe conditions.

The details of the late-term procedures performed at Gosnell's clinic shocked and outraged people around the country—regardless of their views on abortion. Antiabortion groups have used the Gosnell case to push for new restrictions on abortion, particularly late-term procedures. They ask how a procedure done to a living baby outside the womb can be considered first-degree murder, but killing a fetus of the same age before delivery is not. In Washington, DC, the Susan B. Anthony List, an antiabortion nonprofit organization, is pushing for a law that restricts abortions after twenty weeks and plans to push for more federal restrictions as well. "While the nation's attention is turned to this issue, we do think that we need to start having a question about viability and more limits to abortion based on viability nationwide,"[55] says Mallory Quigley, spokeswoman for the Susan B. Anthony List.

Abortion rights supporters say the Gosnell case was an aberration and should not be considered representative of the work done by legal abortion providers, who offer crucial services to women all across the country. Gosnell committed crimes, and for that he deserves to be punished. But, they contend, using this case to impose further restrictions on abortion would punish thousands of women as well. "Justice was served to Kermit Gosnell today and he will pay the price for the atrocities he committed," Ilyse Hogue, president of NARAL Pro-Choice America, said in a statement after the verdict in the Gosnell case. She added this caution: "Anti-choice politicians, and their unrelenting efforts to deny women access to safe and legal abortion care, will only drive more women to back-alley butchers like Kermit Gosnell."[56]

Banning Abortion at Twenty Weeks

Since the details of the Gosnell case emerged, lawmakers in several states have introduced legislation to make late-term abortion illegal. And in June 2013 the US House of Representatives passed a bill that would impose a nationwide ban on nearly all abortions performed after twenty weeks, with exceptions for cases of rape or incest or to save a woman's life. "After this Kermit Gosnell trial and some of the horrific acts that were going on, a vast majority of the American people believe in the substance of this bill and so do I,"[57] House speaker John Boehner of Ohio said about its passage.

Opponents of the bill argue that it is unconstitutional. "The bill bans abortions prior to 20 weeks," says Jerrold Nadler, US representative from New York, ranking member of the Constitution Subcommittee of the House Judiciary Committee. "Since *Roe v. Wade,* it has been well-settled law that no bill is constitutional that bans abortions before viability, which is later than that."[58] Few people believe that the House bill will become law, as it is unlikely to pass the Senate or be signed by President Barack Obama.

Regardless of the outcome, the House bill has inspired debate over late-term abortions. Currently, federal law under *Roe v. Wade* legalizes abortions for all

"The bill bans abortions prior to 20 weeks. Since *Roe v. Wade*, it has been well-settled law that no bill is constitutional that bans abortions before viability, which is later than that."[58]

— US representative Jerrold Nadler of New York.

women until the point of fetal viability. However, determining when a fetus becomes viable is not always clear and can vary from pregnancy to pregnancy. When and under what circumstances, if any, should late-term abortions be permitted? And at what point does the interest of the fetus outweigh the interest of the mother?

Dr. Kermit Gosnell (far left) and his attorney appear in court for sentencing in 2013. Gosnell was convicted of murder and performing abortions after twenty-four weeks, the point at which they are banned in Pennsylvania.

What Is Late-Term Abortion?

An abortion is generally considered to be late-term if it is performed during the later stages of the second trimester (13 to 26 weeks) and anytime during the third trimester (27 to 40 weeks) of pregnancy. Late-term abortions have been more controversial than abortions performed earlier in pregnancy because in the later stages, the fetus is more developed and can potentially be viable outside the womb.

Cost of Abortion

Sometimes women delay having an abortion for a simple reason: They cannot afford it. Under the Hyde Amendment passed in 1977, federal Medicaid funding cannot pay for abortion except in cases of rape, incest, or danger to the woman's life. Several states also have similar laws that restrict financial help to women who seek an abortion. As a result, according to the National Abortion Federation, more than two-thirds of women pay for abortions themselves. Fourteen percent of abortions are paid by state public funds; 13 percent are covered by private insurance. According to the Guttmacher Institute, the average cost of a first-trimester abortion was $470 in 2009, the most recent available data. Without financial assistance, women who choose abortion must wait until they get the money, which often leads to the procedure being postponed until later in the pregnancy.

Although controversial, late-term abortions are very rare in the United States. According to a 2012 report from the Centers for Disease Control and Prevention (CDC), the overwhelming majority of abortions, 91.7 percent, are performed before thirteen weeks gestation. Less than 1.3 percent of abortions are performed at twenty-one weeks gestation or later.

Women undergo late-term abortions for a variety of reasons. In some cases, a woman facing an unplanned pregnancy does not realize that she is pregnant until many weeks have passed. Other times a woman is conflicted about whether or not to continue with a pregnancy and has difficulty making a decision. Sometimes women may encounter difficulty in finding an abortion provider or getting the money to pay for the procedure. Among the most common reasons for delaying an abortion until the second trimester, according to one Guttmacher Institute study, are that it takes a long time to make the arrangements for the procedure (67 percent), it was a hard decision to make (50 percent), and women were late discovering that they were pregnant (36 percent).

In rare but serious cases, doctors may recommend a late-term abortion to save a woman's life or to prevent serious damage to her health. In Ireland, a late-term abortion might have saved the life of Savita Halappanaver, a young married woman, in 2012. When she was seventeen weeks pregnant she went to the hospital for severe back pain and learned that she was miscarrying the fetus. Ireland has a near total ban on abortion, and the hospital refused to abort the fetus even though it had no chance of survival. Doctors denied Savita an abortion for three days, until the fetal heartbeat stopped. At that point Savita had developed severe blood poisoning, and her heart, kidneys, and liver began to fail. Seven days after being denied an abortion, Savita died.

Other women choose to have a late-term abortion after problems with the fetus are discovered. As medical technology has improved, routine ultrasounds are often performed when a woman is eighteen to twenty weeks into her pregnancy. With these tests doctors have been able to diagnose more fetal abnormalities during pregnancy. If a woman chooses to abort the fetus because of the abnormality, it would be a late-term procedure at that point. These cases, however, are rare. In the earlier Guttmacher Institute study, only 1 percent of second trimester abortion patients stated fetal abnormality as a reason for having a late-term abortion.

A Heartbreaking Decision

The decision to have a late-term abortion when a fetal abnormality is discovered can be devastating. When Judy Nicastro discovered that she was pregnant with twins, a boy and a girl, she and her husband were thrilled. In her twentieth week of pregnancy Nicastro had a routine ultrasound. When the technician had a hard time seeing the heart of the male fetus, her doctor ordered a second ultrasound. After the test the Nicastros received devastating news. Doctors suspected the fetus had a herniated diaphragm. His abdominal organs were pushed into his chest and not developing. An MRI scan confirmed the diagnosis. Nicastro endured ten more days of testing and meetings, hoping that there was something doctors could do to save the fetus and give him a good quality of life. Finally, Nicastro and her husband met with staff at the pediatric hospital who told them that the fetus only had one lung chamber formed, and it was only about 20 percent complete. If the fetus survived birth, he probably would be dependent on oxygen and other life supports for the rest of his life. Nicastro and her husband were devastated and decided to proceed with a late-term abortion, at twenty-three weeks. "The next day, at a clinic near my home, I felt my son's budding life end as a doctor inserted a needle through my belly into his tiny heart. She had trouble finding it because of its abnormal position. As horrible as that moment was—it will live with me forever—I am grateful. We made sure our son was not born only to suffer. He died in a warm and loving place, inside me,"[59] says Nicastro.

Nicastro believes that the decision to terminate a pregnancy is an individual choice, based on individual circumstances. "Second-trimester abortions must remain legal because, until a child is viable outside the womb, these decisions belong with the mother. I don't know if *Roe v. Wade* will be overturned in my lifetime, but the chipping away of abortion rights is occurring at an astounding pace. I share my story in the hope that our leaders will be more responsible and compassionate when they weigh what it means to truly value the lives of women and children,"[60] she writes in a 2013 editorial for the *New York Times*.

> "Second-trimester abortions must remain legal because, until a child is viable outside the womb, these decisions belong with the mother."[60]
>
> — Judy Nicastro, who underwent a late-term abortion after her fetus was diagnosed with a serious defect.

Imperfect Fetal Diagnosis

Medical technology allows doctors to see inside the womb during pregnancy, but sometimes it is difficult to correctly interpret what they are seeing in the images. In some cases an ultrasound can indicate a problem even though there is no problem. "Ultrasound is imperfect and analysis of the images can result in inaccurate interpretations. Pregnant women who have declined abortion for fetuses diagnosed by ultrasound with fatal birth defects such as Potter's syndrome (kidney disease with no amniotic fluid)

Willie Parker, Late-Term Abortion Provider

Willie Parker is a late-term abortion provider based in Washington, DC, and Philadelphia. He also travels monthly to see patients in Alabama. An obstetrician for twenty years, Parker began performing abortions in 2004. He says that he began providing abortion services because he was concerned that women's health needs were not being met. When asked about new bans on abortion after twenty weeks, Parker says, "Because of the later stage of development, these are people who are banking on blurring lines around viability. I think it's a very calculated strategy that fails to take into account the complexity of these cases. I think it's also unfortunate, because it vilifies the women who might need an abortion the most."

Parker also believes that laws that ban late-term abortions put providers in a complicated situation. "These laws put providers in a position where they have to turn away patients who have great need. I also think they create this impression that abortion providers are callous, and allow people to conflate murder and abortion. People feel morally justified to say 'this is wrong' because they're led to think it's close to murder. I think that jeopardizes us, by conflating abortion with an issue that would cause moral outrage," he says.

Quoted in Sarah Kliff, "An Interview with a Late Term Abortion Provider," *Washington Post*, May 19, 2012. www.washingtonpost.com.

or thanatophoric dwarfism (a fatal form of skeletal disease), have sometimes ended up giving birth to normal babies,"[61] says Mary L. Davenport, a California obstetrician/gynecologist and former president of the American Association of Pro-Life Obstetricians and Gynecologists.

In other cases fetuses diagnosed with serious anatomical problems and other severe birth defects have had successful surgical repair after birth. At eighteen weeks, a routine ultrasound revealed that Maureen and Kenny Simoncini's baby had a serious medical condition called omphalocele, a birth defect that causes the abdominal organs to protrude into the base of the umbilical cord. "Once it was established that our baby had an omphalocele, we were transferred to a doctor at our local hospital who specialized in high-risk pregnancies. It soon became clear that our case was severe—on more than one occasion we were told that our baby's chances of survival were minimal at best,"[62] says Maureen Simoncini.

The Simoncinis did not consider aborting their baby to be an option. Instead they met with specialists at Boston Children's Hospital who developed a plan for the baby. A few months later, Maureen gave birth to Brody, who was immediately transferred to Boston Children's Hospital so that doctors could begin his treatment. Like many babies born with an omphalocele, Brody had several other serious medical concerns that also needed treatment. For the next seven and a half months, Brody remained in the hospital while doctors corrected his birth defects, one at a time. He had a stent placed in his heart to improve blood flow, underwent open-heart surgery to repair an atrial septal defect, and had a tracheostomy to improve his breathing. To close his omphalocele, doctors placed Brody in a coma and stitched a special man-made material over his exposed organs. Over time, the organs were pushed back into his abdomen. "Brody's just had his first birthday, a milestone we sometimes wondered if he'd ever see. He's thrived so much in the past few months it's almost like he's a different person,"[63] says Maureen.

Alternatives to Late-Term Abortion

Even in cases of fatal fetal defects, those who oppose abortion say that there are more humane alternatives. "For fatal birth defects, abortion is sometimes presented as the only option. But a better alternative is perinatal hospice. This involves continuing the pregnancy until labor begins and giving birth normally, in a setting of comfort and support until natural death occurs. It is similar to what is done for families with terminally ill children and adults,"[64] says Davenport.

Nineteen weeks into her pregnancy, Jenny Mohler and her husband discovered through an ultrasound that the child she carried had a rare disorder that prevented the rib cage from growing, which smothered the fetus's heart and lungs. Doctors told the couple that the baby would likely be stillborn or would die shortly after birth. Despite the grim outlook, Mohler said that termination was never an option for her. She turned to Gilchrist Kids, a division of Gilchrist Hospice Care based in Towson, Maryland, which had a perinatal focus. They talked with social worker Briana Shirey who provided comfort to the couple, prepared them for the months to come, and encouraged them to bond with their unborn son.

When their son was delivered via C-section, he was born alive. He lived for one hour, during which time the Mohlers held

Ultrasounds are routinely done to monitor the health of the fetus throughout pregnancy (as shown). In rare cases, late in pregnancy, they can also help doctors identify serious problems which might lead to a late-term abortion.

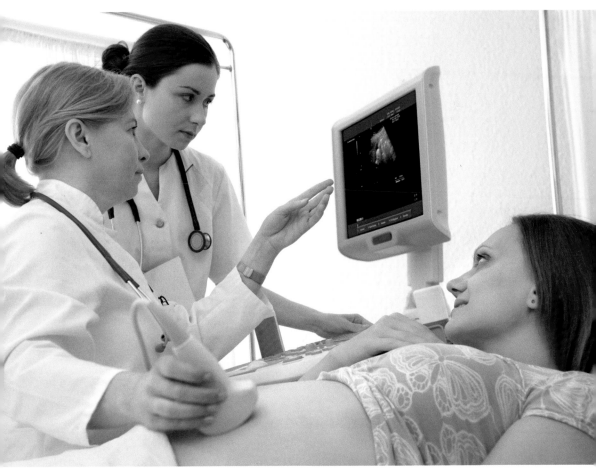

him, took pictures and made molds of his feet and hands. He died peacefully, in their arms. The Mohlers say that the hospice program helped them prepare for their son's death. "I know most people would expect us to say the most difficult day was the day of his death, but to be honest, it wasn't at all," Jenny Mohler says. "December 13th was an amazingly grace-filled and peaceful day full of love. Because we had good care and we were prepared, the hour we spent with our son was truly one of the most beautiful and meaningful of my life."[65]

The Question of Fetal Viability

The prevailing medical opinion at the time of the *Roe v. Wade* decision was that a fetus could survive outside the womb at around twenty-eight weeks or possibly as early as twenty-four weeks. But medical technology and knowledge have advanced significantly since 1973. Greater numbers of premature babies are surviving and thriving at earlier ages—in some cases as early as twenty-three to twenty-four weeks. This raises questions about the legal standard used to determine fetal viability.

The earlier a baby is born, the higher the risk of serious health problems because his or her body has not yet fully developed. Many babies born before thirty-four weeks have breathing problems because their lungs do not have a protein called surfactant that keeps small air sacs in the lungs from collapsing. Premature babies are also at risk of bleeding in the brain or heart failure. Because their immune systems are not fully formed, they have a higher risk of developing infections.

Over the years improvements in medical care and technology have increased the survival rate of premature babies and pushed the potential for fetal viability earlier. Medical specialists care for premature babies in state-of-the-art neonatal intensive care units. They give premature babies surfactant that matures their lungs and administer steroids before delivery to pregnant women at risk of a preterm birth to mature the baby's lungs and decrease the risk of bleeding in the brain. According to a 2009 study by researchers at Lund University in Sweden, 53 percent of babies born at twenty-three weeks who received aggressive medical care survived past the age of one, when the study concluded. Survival rates increased to 67 percent at 24 weeks, 82 percent at 25 weeks, and 85 percent at 26 weeks. "The most important finding in this study is the high survival of extremely preterm infants born alive,"[66] write the study's authors. Study researchers plan to conduct follow-up studies on the babies to follow their growth and survival in the future.

In another study, British researchers from Queen Mary University of London, the UCL Elizabeth Garrett Anderson Institute for Women's Health, and the University of Leicester reported in 2012 that over an eleven-year period, there was an increase in survival rates for babies born extremely prematurely, between twenty-two and twenty-six weeks. In 1995, 40 percent of these extremely premature babies survived and were well enough to leave the hospital, while in 2006 the survival rate increased to 53 percent. The researchers credited medical developments such as giving the pregnant woman steroids to prepare a baby's lungs for premature birth with increasing survival rates.

States Move to Restrict Late-Term Abortions

Although federal law currently permits late-term abortions, *Roe v. Wade* held that states may ban or restrict abortions after fetal viability provided that these policies meet certain requirements. According to the Guttmacher Institute, as of July 2013 forty-one states ban some abortions after a certain point in pregnancy. Of these, twenty-two states prohibit abortion after fetal viability, four states prohibit abortion in the third trimester, and fifteen states impose restrictions after a certain number of weeks. Eight of the latter group define late-term as twenty weeks, or even at the first sign of a heartbeat (which can be as early as six weeks).

In many cases the courts have struck down state restrictions on late-term abortion, often because the restrictions did not have an exception for the woman's health, or the existing health exception was too limited. For example, a federal district court ruled in 2001 that Alabama's abortion ban was unconstitutional because it lacked a health exception and imposed an undue burden on a woman's right to abortion. The courts have also struck down state restrictions that establish fetal viability as a pre-determined number of weeks instead of an individual case-by-case determination by a physician. In 2013 a federal court struck down Arizona's ban on abortion after twenty weeks of pregnancy. The court ruled that the law violated a woman's constitutional right to end a pregnancy before the fetus is viable outside the womb. Still, several state regulations that directly oppose federal law remain in force in some states. For example, in Michigan post-viability abortion is only permitted if the woman's life is in serious danger. In states such as Arkansas late-term abortions are banned after twenty weeks regardless of any possible threat to the health of the mother.

Partial-Birth Abortions

Although late-term abortions are permitted under federal law, one form of late-term abortion known as partial-birth abortion is prohibited. In 2003 President George W. Bush signed the Partial Birth Abortion Ban Act of 2003, the first federal law banning partial-birth abortions. Partial-birth abortion describes a procedure known in the medical community as dilation and extraction. The procedure terminates a pregnancy by partially extracting a fetus from the woman's uterus, then collapsing its skull and removing its brain. The dilation and extraction procedure is usually performed later in pregnancy, often between twenty to twenty-four weeks.

A few years earlier, in 2000, the Supreme Court had struck down a Nebraska law that prohibited partial-birth abortions, in *Stenberg v. Carhart*. The court ruled that the Nebraska law did not include a necessary exception to preserve the woman's health and determined that states did not have the right to endanger a woman's health when regulating abortion methods. In addition, the majority found that the wording of the Nebraska ban was unclear and could be interpreted by doctors to include other abortion methods, which would impose an undue burden on a woman's ability to have an abortion.

In 2007 the issue of partial birth abortion again came before

"I am pleased that the Supreme Court upheld a law that prohibits the abhorrent procedure of partial-birth abortion. . . . The Supreme Court's decision is an affirmation of the progress we have made over the past six years in protecting human dignity and upholding the sanctity of life."[67]

— Former US president George W. Bush.

the Supreme Court in *Gonzales v. Carhart*, which challenged the 2003 federal ban. This time, however, the Supreme Court reversed its position on the issue and upheld the federal ban by a vote of five to four. The court declared that the federal statute was constitutional even though it did not have an exception for cases in which a woman's health was in danger. This was a significant change from other court rulings, which had previously struck down laws that did not contain a similar exception. In response to the court's ruling, President George W. Bush released a statement expressing his agreement with the decision, "I am pleased that the Supreme Court upheld a law that prohibits the abhorrent procedure of partial-birth abortion. . . . The Supreme Court's decision is an affirmation of the progress we have made over the past six years in protecting human dignity and upholding the sanctity of life. We will continue to work for the day when every child is welcomed in life and protected in law."[67]

> "I think most Americans are uncomfortable with late-term abortions."[69]
>
> — Rick Santorum, former US senator from Pennsylvania.

Abortion-rights advocates condemned the 2003 Act and the Supreme Court ruling as the first steps toward trying to make all abortions illegal. Without a health exception, a woman could be forced to carry a fetus that has no chance at life or to continue a pregnancy that jeopardizes her health, leaving her unable to bear children in the future or worsening serious conditions such as diabetes. In her dissenting opinion, Justice Ruth Bader Ginsburg writes,

> Today's decision is alarming. . . . It tolerates, indeed applauds, federal intervention to ban nationwide a procedure found necessary and proper in certain cases by the American College of Obstetricians and Gynecologists (ACOG). It blurs the line, firmly drawn in *Casey*, between previability and postviability abortions. And, for the first time since *Roe*, the Court blesses a prohibition with no exception safeguarding a woman's health. . . . In candor, the Act, and the Court's defense of it, cannot be understood as anything other than an effort to chip away at a right declared again and again by this Court.[68]

Where to Draw the Line?

While the majority of Americans believe that abortion should be legal, as a pregnancy progresses many become uncomfortable with the idea of late-term abortion. According to a December 2012 Gallup poll, the majority of Americans, 61 percent, believe that abortion should be legal in the first trimester of pregnancy. Support for the procedure declines as the pregnancy progresses. According to the same poll, only 27 percent of Americans support second-trimester abortions, and even less, 14 percent, support third-trimester abortions. "I think most Americans are uncomfortable with late-term abortions," says Rick Santorum, former US senator from Pennsylvania. "Where do you draw the line?"[69]

Facts

- Only 11 percent of all abortion providers offer abortions at twenty-four weeks, according to the Guttmacher Institute.

- Fifty-eight percent of abortion patients say they would have liked to have had their abortion earlier, according to the Guttmacher Institute.

- Nearly 60 percent of women who experienced a delay in obtaining an abortion cite the reason as the time it took to make arrangements and raise money, reports the Guttmacher Institute.

- The risk of death associated with abortion increases with the length of pregnancy, from one death for every 1 million abortions at or before eight weeks to one per 29,000 at sixteen to twenty weeks, and one per 11,000 at twenty-one or more weeks, according to the Orlando Women's Center.

What Measures Will Reduce the Need for Abortion?

Although people may vehemently disagree over the moral and legal issues surrounding abortion, most believe that reducing abortions is a goal that benefits both individuals and society as a whole. Instead of focusing on efforts to reduce abortion access, addressing the problem earlier—before a woman is faced with the difficult decision of whether or not to terminate a pregnancy—may be a more effective approach. This idea has spurred efforts to reduce the number of unintended pregnancies, increase access to effective and affordable birth control, and provide better support for mothers and children. While some people support one method over another, many believe that a combination of several approaches may be the most effective way to reduce abortions in the United States.

Reducing Unintended Pregnancy

Unintended pregnancies are common in the United States. Nearly half of all pregnancies are unintended, according to 2013 statistics from the Guttmacher Institute. An unintended pregnancy is one that is mistimed, unplanned, or unwanted at conception, and it

Adoption Alternative

In 2012 Heroic Media, a pro-life media group, and Bethany Christian Services, a national adoption agency, joined to launch the first national television campaign that urged women to choose adoption over abortion. Over a four-week period, approximately forty-five television spots aired on the Oxygen Network. The response to the ads was positive, with Bethany Christian Services receiving hundreds of calls from pregnant women who wanted to learn more about adoption. "Adoption is the overlooked option; less than 1 percent of women with unplanned pregnancies choose adoption, but for every adoptive baby there are 30 to 40 couples waiting to welcome the child into their family," says Marissa Cope, director of Marketing, Communications and Research at Heroic Media. "Heroic Media's mission is to present women with hopeful alternatives to abortion—and adoption is a beautiful alternative," the production group added. "Our new pro-adoption TV commercial shares the message that adoption is a loving choice that gives a birth mother the ability to choose a family for her baby and receive support throughout her pregnancy."

Quoted in Christian News Network, "Pro-Life Media Group and Adoption Agency Making Impact with National Ad Offering Abortion Alternative," January 7, 2013. http://christiannews.net.

is more likely to be terminated than an intended pregnancy. According to the Guttmacher Institute, four out of ten unintended pregnancies end in abortion. Knowing these statistics, many people believe that reducing the incidence of unintended pregnancy will lead to fewer abortions. That means targeting the factors that most often contribute to unintended pregnancies. These include failure to use contraception, not using contraception correctly or consistently, and relying on less effective methods of contraception, such as withdrawal or ovulation-cycle monitoring. Several measures have been proposed to reduce unintended pregnancies. Some communities and organizations have created mass media campaigns designed to educate the public about the consequences of unprotected sex and provide information about contraception options and proper use. According to the Brookings Institution, which looked at mass media campaigns that urged men and women of all ages to avoid unprotected sex, a well-designed campaign can encourage changes in behavior by about 3 to 6 percent of the target group, which in turn can lead to fewer unplanned pregnancies and thereby reduce the need for abortions.

In 2011 the National Campaign to Prevent Teen and Unplanned Pregnancy debuted a national multimedia public service campaign designed to reduce the rates of unplanned pregnancy among older teens and young adults. The campaign aims to help sexually active women aged eighteen to twenty-four find the right birth control method and use it correctly and consistently. The program uses a series of online, video, and mobile components where young adults can explore and compare different methods of contraception, watch videos of other young adults' personal experiences, and watch short animated clips about birth control. In addition, the campaign engages young adults on social media through Facebook and Twitter sites. "Despite the public's perception that unplanned pregnancy is largely confined to teens, new research reveals that this issue is a major problem among young adults and the consequences can be very serious," says Peggy Conlon, president and CEO of the Ad Council. "This breakthrough ad campaign uses identifiable humor to empower young women to find the birth control method that is best for them. It's a public health effort that has the potential to benefit many, many young women."[70]

Youth Pregnancy Prevention

In addition to mass media advertising, pregnancy prevention programs in communities and schools that target teens and young adults can reduce unintended pregnancy rates. These programs give young people information about how to protect themselves from unintended pregnancy. Some emphasize abstinence as the

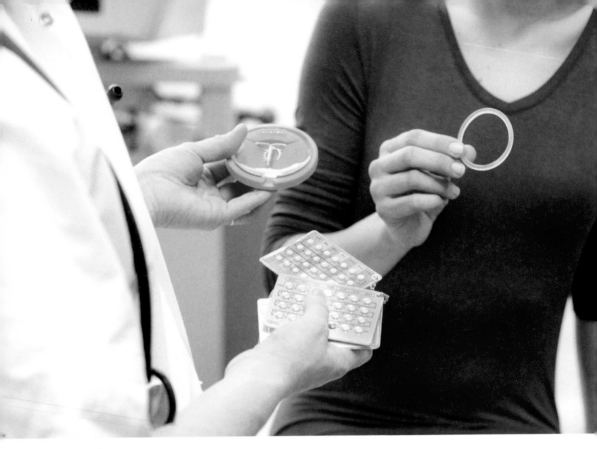

One way to reduce the need for abortion is to make sure people have access to contraception. Many methods of birth control are available, although some are more costly—and more effective—than others.

only 100 percent certain method to avoid pregnancy, while also educating youth about how to use different types of contraception. According to the Brookings Institution, pregnancy prevention programs can reduce sexual activity by 15 percent or more and increase contraception use by 25 percent or more.

Prime Time is an eighteen-month program designed by the University of Minnesota Prevention Research Center to prevent teen pregnancy. The program operates at a primary care clinic and aims to change girls' sexual risk behavior by providing mentoring and counseling and helping them set personal goals. Girls in the program meet with case managers monthly on a one-on-one basis to talk about healthy relationships, responsible sexual behavior, and positive family and school involvement. They also participate in weekly peer group discussions.

To evaluate the program, researchers studied 253 sexually active girls aged thirteen to seventeen. Half were assigned to the

Prime Time program, while the other half received no special counseling or support. Six months after the completion of the program, researchers found that girls in the Prime Time program reported significantly more consistent use of condoms, birth control pills, or a combination of the two as compared to the girls who were not in the program. The girls in the program also reported increased family connectedness, self-confidence, and a reduction in the perceived importance of having sexual intercourse. "Findings suggest that health services grounded in a youth development framework can lead to long-term reductions in sexual risk among vulnerable youth,"[71] the Prime Time study authors write.

The Problem of Cost

Consistent and accurate use of contraceptives is one of the most effective ways to reduce unintended pregnancy and demand for abortions. Yet the high cost of effective contraception and limited access for many women reduces the use of contraception and leads to more unintended pregnancies, according to research from the Brookings Institution. Many of the most effective methods of contraception, including the birth control pill, intrauterine devices, and birth control patches and injections are expensive. For example, intrauterine devices (IUDs) can cost about $750 to $850. Birth control pills can amount to anywhere from $160 to $600 a year. Both of these methods also require periodic visits with a health care professional. Alternatively, condoms are a less expensive form of birth control ($1 each) that is easily available at drugstores. Yet condoms are less reliable, with 2 percent of couples who use them properly becoming pregnant and 18 percent becoming pregnant if they do not use them correctly, as compared to less than 1 percent of women who become pregnant while using an IUD.

Issues related to cost lead many women to stop or delay using their preferred method of contraception, according to the Center for American Progress, an independent nonpartisan education institute. Others choose less effective contraception, such as condoms, because it is more affordable. A survey by the Guttmacher Institute found that to save money, nearly one in four women with household income of less than $75,000 put off a doctor's visit for birth control in the past year, while 25 percent of pill users saved money by inconsistent use.

Making contraception affordable and accessible to women across the country, particularly those in low-income households, can decrease the number of un-intended pregnancies and resulting abortions. A study published in 2010 in the journal *Obstetrics and Gynecology* found that providing free, reliable birth control could prevent between 41 percent and 71 percent of abortions in the United States. In the study, researchers recruited more than nine thousand teens and adult women in the St. Louis, Missouri, area. They provided the women with free, effective, reversible birth control such as pills, vaginal rings, patches, or intrauterine devices and implants. Researchers found that the teen birth rate and the overall abortion rate for participants dropped. The teen birth rate was 6.3 per 1,000 women in the study as compared to the national teen birth rate of 34.3 per 1,000 women. The abortion rate was 4.4 to 7.5 per 1,000 women, less than half the national abortion rate of 19.6 per 1,000 women. "The impact of providing no-cost birth control was far greater than we expected,"[72] says Jeff Peipert, a professor of obstetrics and gynecology at Washington University in St. Louis and study coauthor.

The researchers estimate that if a similar program were implemented nationwide, more than one million annual abortions could be avoided. "We think improving access to birth control, particularly IUDs and [hormone] implants, coupled with education on the most effective methods, has the potential to significantly decrease the number of unintended pregnancies and abortions in this country,"[73] says Peipert.

Contraceptive Coverage Under the Affordable Care Act

In 2012 the US Congress took a step to make contraception more affordable when it passed the Affordable Care Act, which includes a mandate that all new insurance policies must provide birth control

Abortion Pill or Emergency Contraception?

While emergency contraception is an alternative to abortion, it is often confused with medication abortion or the abortion pill. First introduced as RU-486, the abortion pill can terminate a pregnancy up to sixty-three days after a woman's last menstruation. It works by blocking the hormones necessary to maintain a pregnancy. Then another medication called misoprostol causes the woman's uterus to contract and empty. In contrast, emergency contraception prevents pregnancy before it occurs by limiting ovulation and fertilization.

One type of emergency contraception, called ella, has sparked debate between the pro-choice and pro-life communities. The drug is sold as emergency contraception and is intended to be used to prevent pregnancy for up to five days after unprotected sex. Because the drug is similar chemically to the abortion pill, some believe that it could also induce abortion. "[Ella] is an abortion drug," says Wendy Wright, president of Concerned Women for America. "It operates the same way as RU-486, which is an abortion drug. Many women may be comfortable taking a contraceptive but would object to taking an abortion drug."

The drug's manufacturer however, insists that it is not an abortion pill. "We're very clear on the fact that this is indeed a contraceptive—a method of prevention of pregnancy," says Erin Gainer, chief executive of HRA Pharma of Paris.

Quoted in CBN.com, "Ella One: America's New Abortion Drug?," August 16, 2010. www.cbn.com.

Quoted in Rob Stein, "New 'Morning-After' pill, Ella, Raises Debate Over Similarity to Abortion Drug," *Washington Post*, June 12, 2010. www.washingtonpost.com.

with no copayment. "The health care law helps ensure that millions of women have coverage for critical preventive services without cost sharing," says Chiquita Brooks-LaSure, deputy director of policy and regulation at the Center for Consumer Information, part of the US Department of Health and Human Services. These services include contraception "because there are tremendous health benefits for women that come from using contraception,"[74] she says.

The mandate was met with fierce protest from some churches, religious organizations, and other conservatives who hold strong beliefs against the use of contraceptives. They also argue that greater access to contraceptives does not decrease the number of abortions. According to the United States Conference of Catholic Bishops, contraceptives often fail to prevent pregnancy because many people use them incorrectly or not all the time. As a result, 48 percent of women who experience unintended pregnancies and 54 percent of women seeking abortion used contraception in the month they became pregnant. In addition, they point to a study in Spain that studied contraceptive use and abortions over a ten-year period from 1997 to 2007. Published in the journal *Contraception* in January 2011, the Spanish researchers found that while there was a 63 percent increase in contraceptive use over the period, there was also an unexplained 108 percent increase in the elective abortion rate.

Emergency Contraception

The availability of emergency contraception may also prevent unintended pregnancy and resulting abortions. Emergency contraception is birth control that can be used up to five days after unprotected sex. It generally comes in two forms—the morning-after pill available at health centers and drugstores and the ParaGard IUD insertion available at health centers.

Pregnancy does not always occur immediately after unprotected sex. It can take several days for sperm to fertilize an egg. The morning-after pill works to prevent pregnancy by keeping a woman's ovary from releasing an egg for a longer time than usual. If there is no egg for the sperm to fertilize, pregnancy does not occur. According to Planned Parenthood, morning-after pills are generally up to 89 percent effective at preventing pregnancy when

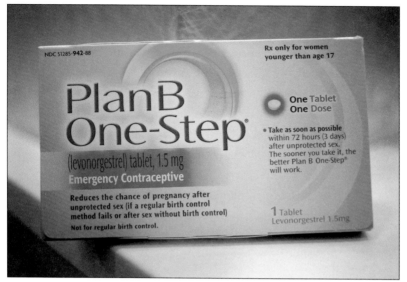

As of 2013, the emergency contraceptive Plan B One-Step is available without a prescription to women of child-bearing age. Taken within seventy-two hours of unprotected sexual intercourse, Plan B disrupts ovulation and thereby prevents pregnancy.

taken within seventy-two hours after unprotected sex. They are less effective as time passes, but still reduce pregnancy risk for up to five days.

In 2013 the US Food and Drug Administration expanded its approval of a single dose morning-after pill, Plan B One-Step, to allow it to be sold over the counter without a prescription or restrictions to all women of childbearing age, in response to an order from a US district court. "Over-the-counter access to emergency contraceptive products has the potential to further decrease the rate of unintended pregnancies in the United States,"[75] says Janet Woodcock, long-time director of the FDA's Center for Drug Evaluation and Research.

Concerns About the Morning-After Pill

Yet many people are uncomfortable with the idea of anyone, especially young teens, being able to purchase the morning-after pill without parental knowledge. "There are two main issues: The first is that we are putting the safety of young girls at risk, and the second is we are trampling on the rights of parents," says Anna Higgins, director of the Center for Human Dignity at the Family Research Council, a Christian nonprofit public policy group. "The effects of taking this high-dose of hormones during puberty have not been studied, so they are unknown. People are assuming it's safe, but we just don't know that. . . . We need to encourage parent-teen communication on the medical and moral issues of sexual behavior." Higgins is also concerned that the availability of emergency contraception will encourage risky teenage sexual activity. "The increased availability of plan B [morning after pill] to teens will increase sexual activity among that age group,"[76] says Higgins.

Critics of emergency contraception argue that it does not reduce unintended pregnancy and abortion. The availability of emergency contraception has also been linked to an increase in risky sexual behavior. In a 2010 study researchers from Nottingham University in England found that access to free emergency contraception encouraged teens to have unprotected sex and did not reduce the number of unintended pregnancies. The researchers compared areas of England where the morning-after pill was available to those where it was not. They found that the pregnancy rates for girls aged sixteen or younger remained the same in both areas, while the rate of sexually transmitted diseases increased by 12 percent in areas where the morning-after pill was available free of charge. "We find that offering the morning-after pill free of charge didn't have the intended effect of cutting teenage pregnancies but did have the unfortunate side of effect of increasing sexually transmitted infections," says David Patton, one of the study researchers. "By focusing on sexually transmitted infections, it allows us to test whether there is an impact on sexual risk-taking, and that seems to be the implication."[77]

Supporting Mothers and Children

Raising a child is an expensive undertaking. According to the latest data from the US Department of Agriculture, parents can expect to spend an average of $235,000 to raise a child born in 2011 to the age of seventeen. For some women these costs are unaffordable, and they turn to abortion. According to the Guttmacher Institute, 75 percent of women who choose abortion say that they cannot afford a child. In addition, 42 percent of women who have abortions have incomes below 100 percent of the federal poverty level.

If women are choosing abortion because they do not have the resources or support to have a child, then another method of reducing the number of abortions may be providing better support to women and their children. "If you're serious about reducing abortion, the most important issue is not which abortions to ban. The most important issue is how will you support women to have the babies they want,"[78] says journalist David Frum. Frum cites Germany as an example of a country that supports women and children and has historically low abortion rates. German woman receive fourteen weeks of maternity leave, paid by the state. The country also pays parents an allowance for every child for as many as twenty-five years, depending on how long the child stays in school. In addition, German women who choose to leave work to stay at home with their children receive a replacement wage from the government for up to fourteen months. As a result, according to the Guttmacher Institute, the German abortion rate is approximately one-third the rate in the United States. "As a general rule, societies that do the most to support mothers and child-bearing have the fewest abortions. Societies that do the least to support mothers and child-bearing have more abortions,"[79] says Frum.

> "The increased availability of plan B [morning after pill] to teens will increase sexual activity among that age group."[76]
>
> — Anna Higgins, director of the Center for Human Dignity at the Family Research Council.

With the aim of supporting pregnant women and their children, the US Congress created the Pregnancy Assistance Fund (PAF) as part of the Affordable Care Act signed into law in 2010. The PAF provides $25 million annual funding to states to provide pregnant and parenting women with supportive services to help them complete education and gain access to health care, child care, housing, and other important supports. "We are encouraged that the government is finally setting aside a small amount of funds in the Pregnancy Assistance Fund to support those women who make the courageous and selfless choice to give life to their babies despite life's challenges,"[80] says Melinda Delahoyde, president of Care Net, an organization that provides abortion alternatives to women.

A young mother in Missouri prepares her daughter for the trip home from daycare. Increased support from government and private organizations might make it possible for some women to have their babies rather than abort them.

A Common Goal

Although Americans may disagree on the best approach to reducing the number of abortions, many efforts in place are having an impact. Nationally, the abortion rate has steadily declined. According to most recent statistics from the Guttmacher Institute, approximately 1.21 million abortions were performed in 2008, down from 1.31 million in 2000. In addition, data from the CDC show that US abortion rates dropped an additional 5 percent between 2008 and 2009, the most recent years with available data. The reasons behind the decline have not been linked to the data, although some experts suggest increasing use of contraceptives, IUDs, and access to emergency contraceptives may have played a role.

David Gushee, a professor of Christian ethics and director of the Center for Theology and Public Life at Mercer University, says that the goal of reducing abortion is something most Americans want, regardless of where they stand on abortion rights issues. "I've always thought that common ground was possible around the conviction that abortion is not a moral good," says Gushee. "A society with over a million abortions a year is not a good thing."[81]

Facts

- Publicly funded family planning services helped women avoid 1.94 million unintended pregnancies in one year, which would likely have resulted in about 860,000 unintended births and 810,000 abortions, according to the Guttmacher Institute.

- Guttmacher Institute research shows that the two-thirds of US women at risk of unintended pregnancy who use contraception consistently and correctly throughout the course of any given year account for only 5 percent of all unintended pregnancies.

- Two of the leading reasons women give for aborting their pregnancy are economic in nature: They cannot afford a child, or they fear a baby would interfere with work, school or other responsibilities, reports Focus on the Family.

- Delaying the initiation of or reducing early sexual activity among teens can decrease their overall exposure to risks of unwed childbearing, STDs, and psycho-emotional harm, says the Heritage Foundation.

- The typical use failure rate of the birth control pill is about 9 percent according to the CDC. The typical use-failure rate for the male condom is about 18 percent.

Source Notes

Introduction: Clashing Beliefs

1. Quoted in Christina Caldwell, "Abortion Heat Hits Alabama's 'Saturday Women,'" Thomson Reuters Foundation, August 11, 2013. www.trust.org.
2. Quoted in Caldwell, "Abortion Heat Hits Alabama's 'Saturday Women.'"
3. Quoted in Karen Tumulty, "Four Decades After *Roe v. Wade*, Views of Most Americans Still Complex, Conditional," *Washington Post*, July 10, 2013. http://articles.washingtonpost.com.

Chapter One: What Are the Origins of the Abortion Controversy?

4. Fourteenth Amendment, United States Constitution. http://memory.loc.gov.
5. Harry Blackmun, majority opinion, *Roe v. Wade*, US Supreme Court, January 22, 1973. www.law.cornell.edu.
6. Byron White, dissenting opinion, *Doe v. Bolton*, US Supreme Court, January 22, 1973. www.law.cornell.edu.
7. Quoted in Bill Mears, "Four Decades After *Roe:* A Legacy of Law and Morality," CNN.com, January 19, 2013. www.cnn.com.
8. Blackmun, majority opinion, *Roe v. Wade*.
9. Quoted in Physicians for Reproductive Health, "Mildred Hanson, MD," *Voices for Change*, August 14, 2008. http://prh.org.
10. Quoted in Julie Rovner, *Roe v. Wade* Turns 40, but Abortion Debate Is Even Older," January 22, 2013, NPR.org. http://m.npr.org/news/Health.
11. Quoted in Julie Rovner, *Roe v. Wade* Turns 40, but Abortion Debate Is Even Older," January 22, 2013, NPR.org. http://m.npr.org/news/Health.
12. Quoted in Julie Rovner, *Roe v. Wade* Turns 40, but Abortion Debate Is Even Older," January 22, 2013, NPR.org. http://m.npr.org/news/Health.
13. National Conference of Catholic Bishops, "Declaration on Abortion," Teachings of the Catholic Church on Abortion, November 18, 1970. http://www.priestsforlife.org.
14. Quoted in Stephanie Pappas, "America & Abortion: Will Controversy Ever Die?," LiveScience.com, November 10, 2011. www.livescience.com.
15. Quoted in David Crary, "Americans Conflicted on Abortion Issue, Survey Shows," Boston.com, June 10, 2011. www.boston.com.

Chapter Two: Is Abortion Moral?

16. Quoted in Crary, "Americans Conflicted on Abortion Issue, Survey Shows."
17. Calum Hayes, "The Abortion Debate: When Does Life Begin?," *Neon Tommy*—Annenberg Digital News, July 9, 2013. www.neontommy.com.
18. Quoted in Alia Beard Rau, "Anti-abortion Leaders Rally in Favor of New Clinic Restrictions," *Arizona Republic*, June 6, 2013. www.azcentral.com.
19. "When Does Life Begin?," National Right to Life. www.nrlc.org.

20. Rick Perry, "Gov. Perry Gives Remarks to the National Right to Life Convention," Office of the Governor: Rick Perry, June 27, 2013. http://governor.state.tx.us.

21. Quoted in CNN.com, "Medical Views: When Does Human Life Begin?," *The Chart* (blog), November 7, 2011. http://thechart.blogs.cnn.com.

22. Quoted in CNN.com, "Medical Views: When Does Human Life Begin?"

23. NARAL Pro Choice Wisconsin, "Anti-Choice Statements—Pro-Choice Responses." www.prochoicewisconsin.org.

24. NARAL Pro Choice Wisconsin, "Anti-Choice Statements—Pro-Choice Responses."

25. Quoted in John Hudson, "The Debate Around Fetal Pain and Abortions," Atlantic Wire, April 14, 2010. www.theatlanticwire.com.

26. Quoted in Values Voter News, "Nebraska Enacts First-Ever Abortion Ban Based on Fetal Pain," April 13, 2010. www.valuesvoternews.com.

27. Quoted in National Right to Life Committee, "Pain of the Unborn Child: What Does an Unborn Child Feel?," www.nrlc.org.

28. Quoted in Mary Wisniewski, "'Fetal Pain' Anti-abortion Laws Spur Fierce Debate," Reuters.com, April 6, 2011. www.reuters.com.

29. Quoted in *ScienceDaily*, "Babies Distinguish Pain from Touch at 35–37 Weeks, Research Finds," September 8, 2011. www.sciencedaily.com.

30. Quoted in *USA Today*, "Idaho First State to Have Fetal Pain Law Rejected," March 7, 2013. www.usatoday.com.

31. Mary Elizabeth Williams, "I Believe That Life Starts at Conception. And It's Never Stopped Me from Being Pro-Choice," *Salon*, January 23, 2013. www.salon.com.

32. Quoted in Kim Painter, "Doctors Say Abortions Do Sometimes Save Women's Lives," *USA Today*, October 22, 2012. www.usatoday.com.

33. Quoted in Painter, "Doctors Say Abortions Do Sometimes Save Women's Lives."

34. Quoted in Painter, "Doctors Say Abortions Do Sometimes Save Women's Lives."

35. Quoted in Associated Press in NBC News, "AP: Man Admits Killing Kansas Abortion Doctor," November 9, 2009. www.nbcnews.com.

36. Quoted in Joe Stumpe and Monica Davey, "Abortion Doctor Shot to Death in Kansas Church," *New York Times*, May 31, 2009. www.nytimes.com.

37. Quoted in Public Religion Research Institute, "Millennial Generation Committed to Availability, Conflicted About Morality of Abortion," news release, June 9, 2011. http://publicreligion.org.

Chapter Three: Should States Have the Right to Place Limits on Abortion?

38. Quoted in John Eligon and Erik Eckholm, "New Laws Ban Most Abortions in North Dakota," *New York Times*, March 26, 2013. www.nytimes.com.

39. Quoted in Eligon and Eckholm, "New Laws Ban Most Abortions in North Dakota."

40. Quoted in Center for Reproductive Rights, "North Dakota Governor Signs the Nation's Most Extreme Attack on Women's Constitutional Rights into Law," March 26, 2013. http://reproductiverights.org.

41. Quoted in Rob Christensen, John Frank, and Caitlin Owens, "McCrory Voices Concern Over Abortion Bill Passed by the Senate," Newsobserver.com, July 8, 2013. www.newsobserver.com.

42. Quoted in Christensen, Frank, and Owens, "McCrory Voices Concern Over Abortion Bill Passed by the Senate."

43. Quoted in Christensen, Frank, and Owens, "McCrory Voices Concern Over Abortion Bill Passed by the Senate."

44. Quoted in Stephanie Condon, "As More States Restrict Abortion, Fight Rages On," CBS News, July 10, 2013. www.cbsnews.com.

45. Quoted in Associated Press in CBS News, "Judge Temporarily Blocks New Wisconsin Abortion Law," July 9, 2013. www.cbsnews.com.

46. Quoted in Julie Hirschfeld Davis, "'Roe v. Wade' Is State Anti-Abortion Laws' Ultimate Target," *Bloomberg Businessweek*, July 11, 2013. www.businessweek .com.

47. Quoted in Americans United for Life, "AUL Says 8th Edition of Defending Life—the Ultimate Source of Pro-life Legislation—'Is a Game Changer,'" February 21, 2013. www.aul.org.

48. Quoted in Davis, "'Roe v. Wade' Is State Anti-Abortion Laws' Ultimate Target."

49. Quoted in Eligon and Eckholm, "New Laws Ban Most Abortions in North Dakota."

50. Quoted in Fernanda Santos, "Arizona Law on Abortions Struck Down as Restrictive," *New York Times*, May 21, 2013. www.nytimes.com.

51. Quoted in Santos, "Arizona Law on Abortions Struck Down as Restrictive."

52. Quoted in Dave McKinney, "Illinois Supreme Court Ends Challenges to Abortion Law," *Chicago Sun Times*, July 11, 2013. www.suntimes.com.

53. Quoted in McKinney, "Illinois Supreme Court Ends Challenges to Abortion Law."

54. Quoted in Ariel Edwards-Levy, "Abortion Laws Proposed in Some States Would Buck National Trend, Expand Access," *Huffington Post*, April 24, 2012. www .huffingtonpost.com.

Chapter Four: Should Late-Term Abortions Be Banned?

55. Quoted in Josh Leys, "Gosnell Horror Fuels Fight for Abortion Laws," CNN. com, May 14, 2013. www.cnn.com.

56. Quoted in Jon Hurdle and Trip Gabriel, "Philadelphia Abortion Doctor Guilty of Murder in Late-Term Procedures," *New York Times*, May 13, 2013. www .nytimes.com.

57. Quoted in Julie Rovner, "House Passes Bill That Would Ban Abortions After 20 Weeks," NPR.org, June 18, 2013. www.npr.org.

58. Quoted in Rovner, "House Passes Bill That Would Ban Abortions After 20 Weeks."

59. Judy Nicastro, "My Abortion, at 23 Weeks," *New York Times*, June 20, 2013. www.nytimes.com.

60. Nicastro, "My Abortion, at 23 Weeks."

61. Mary L. Davenport, "Is Late-Term Abortion Ever Necessary?" American Association of Pro-Life Obstetricians and Gynecologists. www.aaplog.org.

62. Maureen Simoncini, "Our Patients' Stories: Fixing Brody's Omphalocele," blog, Boston Children's Hospital, March 22, 2013. http://childrenshospitalblog.org.

63. Simoncini, "Our Patients' Stories: Fixing Brody's Omphalocele."

64. Davenport, "Is Late-Term Abortion Ever Necessary?"

65. Quoted in Andrea Walker, "Facing the Death of Baby," *Baltimore Sun*, July 27, 2013. www.baltimoresun.com.

66. Quoted in *ScienceDaily*, "Likelihood of Survival May Be Improving for Extremely Preterm Infants," June 3, 2009. www.sciencedaily.com.

67. George W. Bush, "Statement by the President," White House, April 18, 2007. www.nrlc.org.

68. Ruth Bader Ginsburg, dissenting opinion, "*Gonzales v. Carhart*," April 18, 2007. www.law.cornell.edu.

69. Quoted in James Q. Lynch and Rod Boshart, "Santorum Backs Iowa Move to Ban Late-Term Abortions," *Sioux City (IA) Journal*, June 8, 2011. http://sioux cityjournal.com.

Chapter Five: What Measures Will Reduce the Need for Abortion?

70. Quoted in National Campaign to Prevent Teen and Unplanned Pregnancy, "Nearly One in Ten Unmarried Young Women Has an Unplanned Pregnancy Each Year, According to New Data Released Today," November 10, 2011. www .thenationalcampaign.org.

71. Quoted in Consumer HealthDay, "Teen Pregnancy-Prevention Program Works, Study Says," February 25, 2013. http://consumer.healthday.com.

72. Quoted in Katherine Harmon, "Free Birth Control Access Can Reduce Abortion Rate by More than Half," *Scientific American Blog Network*, October 4, 2012. http://blogs.scientificamerican.com.

73. Quoted in Harmon, "Free Birth Control Access Can Reduce Abortion Rate by More than Half."

74. Quoted in Steve Reinberg and E.J. Mundell, "White House Unveils Final Plan on Coverage for Contraception," *U.S. News & World Report:* "HealthDay," June 28, 2013. http://health.usnews.com.

75. Quoted in Yahoo.com, "FDA Expands "Morning-After" Pill Approval After Court Order," June 20, 2013. http://news.yahoo.com. (Web page no longer available.)

76. Quoted in Nanci Hellmich and Michelle Healy, "Morning-After Pill: The Debate Continues," *USA Today*, June 11, 2013. www.usatoday.com.

77. Quoted in Victoria Ward, "Morning-After Pill Handout Causes Rise in Teenage Sexual Disease, Study Finds," *Telegraph* (London), January 30, 2011. www .telegraph.co.uk.

78. David Frum, "Let's Get Real About Abortions," CNN.com, October 29, 2012. www.cnn.com.

79. Frum, "Let's Get Real About Abortions."

80. Quoted in Penny Starr, "Government's New $25-Million Fund to Help Pregnant Teens May Benefit Abortion Providers, Pro-Family Advocates Say," CNS News, July 12, 2010. www.cnsnews.com.

81. Quoted in John Gehring, "What Ever Happened to the Common Ground on Abortion Reduction?," Religion and Politics, April 16, 2013. http://religionand politics.org.

Related Organizations and Websites

American Civil Liberties Union (ACLU)

125 Broad St., 18th Floor
New York, NY 10004
phone: (212) 549-2500
website: www.aclu.org

The ACLU guards our nation's liberty and works daily in courts, legislatures, and communities to defend and preserve the individual rights and liberties guaranteed under the US Constitution, including the right to personal freedom.

American Life League (ALL)

PO Box 1350
Stafford, VA 22555
phone: (540) 659-4171
fax: (540) 659-2586
website: www.all.org

ALL is a Catholic organization that opposes abortion and sponsors several outreach efforts to focus attention on pro-life issues. ALL provides brochures, videos, and newsletters on its website.

Americans United for Life (AUL)

655 Fifteenth St. NW, Suite 410
Washington, DC 20005
phone: (202) 289-1478
e-mail: info@aul.org
website: www.aul.org

AUL is the country's oldest pro-life organization. It promotes pro-life ideas and policies. Its website includes information about current local and national abortion legislation and ongoing pro-life activities sponsored by the organization.

Center for Reproductive Rights

120 Wall St.
New York, NY 10005
phone: (917) 637-3600
fax: (917) 637-3666
e-mail: info@reprorights.org
website: http://reproductiverights.org

The Center for Reproductive Rights is a global legal advocacy organization dedicated to reproductive rights. The center produces many books, reports, briefing papers, and fact sheets related to reproductive rights issues, including abortion.

Focus on the Family

8605 Explorer Dr.
Colorado Springs, CO 80920-1051
phone: (800) 232-6459
website: www.focusonthefamily.com

Focus on the Family is a nonprofit Christian evangelical organization that works to defend the institution of the family. The group supports pro-life measures and offers books, CDs, and DVDs on many topics, including abortion.

Guttmacher Institute

125 Maiden Lane, 7th Floor
New York, NY 10038
phone: (212) 248-1111
toll-free: (877) 823-0262
fax: (212) 248-1951
website: www.guttmacher.org

The Guttmacher Institute is involved in social science, research policy analysis, and public education for sexual and reproductive health in the United States and worldwide. It produces a wide range of resources on topics involving sexual and reproductive health, including abortion.

NARAL Pro-Choice America

1156 Fifteenth St. NW, Suite 700
Washington, DC 20005
phone: (202) 973-3000
fax: (202) 973-3096
website: www.prochoiceamerica.org

NARAL Pro-Choice America is a leading advocate for privacy and a woman's right to choose. It works to maintain the rights of all women to legal abortion and access to reproductive health care. The organization briefs members of Congress and testifies at hearings on abortion and related issues.

National Abortion Federation (NAF)

1660 L St. NW, Suite 450
Washington, DC 20036
phone: (202) 667-5881
fax: (202) 667-5890
e-mail: naf@prochoice.org
website: http://prochoice.org

The National Abortion Federation is a professional association of abortion providers in the United States and Canada. It publishes numerous resources covering a wide range of subjects related to abortion for health care providers, medical educators, patients, and the public.

National Organization for Women (NOW)

1100 H St. NW, Suite 300
Washington, DC 20005
phone: (202) 628-8669
website: www.now.org

The National Organization for Women is a feminist advocacy organization that seeks equality for all women. One of NOW's top-priority issues is advancing reproductive freedom, including legal abortion.

National Right to Life Committee (NRLC)

512 Tenth St. NW
Washington, DC 20004
phone: (202) 626-8800
e-mail: nrlc@nrlc.org
website: www.nrlc.org

The NRLC was founded in 1973 in response to the US Supreme Court's *Roe v. Wade* decision, which legalized abortion across the country. It is one of the largest antiabortion organizations and works to achieve legislative reform at the national level.

Planned Parenthood Federation of America (PPFA)

434 W. Thirty-Third St.
New York, NY 10001
phone: (212) 541-7800
toll-free (800) 230-7526
fax: (212) 245-1845
website: www.plannedparenthood.org

Founded in 1916, PPFA is a national organization that supports each individual's right to make decisions about health, sex, and family planning. It provides contraception, abortion, reproductive health care, sex education, and related information at health centers across the United States.

Susan B. Anthony List

1707 L St. NW, Suite 550
Washington, DC 20036
phone: 202-223-8073
fax: 202-223-8078
website: www.sba-list.org

The Susan B. Anthony List is an antiabortion organization that is dedicated to electing candidates and pursuing policies that will reduce and ultimately end abortion. The SBA List emphasizes the election, education, promotion, and mobilization of pro-life women.

Additional Reading

Books

Noah Berlatsky, ed., *Abortion: Global Viewpoints*. Farmington Hills, MI: Greenhaven, 2010.

Linda Greenhouse and Reva Siegel, eds., *Before* Roe v. Wade: *Voices that Shaped the Abortion Debate Before the Supreme Court's Ruling*. New York: Kaplan, 2010.

David M. Haugen, ed. *Abortion*. Farmington Hills, MI: Greenhaven, 2010.

Melissa Higgins and Joseph W. Dellapenna, Roe v. Wade: *Abortion and a Woman's Right to Privacy*. Minneapolis, MN: ABDO, 2013.

Noël Merino, ed., *Abortion*. Farmington Hills, MI: Greenhaven, 2013.

Tamara Roleff, ed., *Are Abortion Rights Threatened?* Farmington Hills, MI: Greenhaven, 2013.

Stephen Singular, *The Wichita Divide: The Murder of Dr. George Tiller and the Battle over Abortion*. New York: St. Martin's, 2011.

Internet Sources

Rachel Benson Gold and Elizabeth Nash, "TRAP Laws Gain Political Traction While Abortion Clinics—and the Women They Serve—Pay the Price," Guttmacher Policy Review, Spring 2013. www.guttmacher.org/pubs/gpr/16/2/gpr160207.html.

Guttmacher Institute, "An Overview of Abortion Laws," October 1, 2013. www.guttmacher.org/statecenter/spibs/spib_OAL.pdf.

Guttmacher Institute, "State Facts About Abortion," January 2011. www.guttmacher.org/statecenter/sfaa.html.

Bill Mears, "Four Decades After *Roe:* A Legacy of Law and Morality," CNN.com, January 19, 2013. www.cnn.com/2013/01/19/justice/scotus-roe-anniversary.

National Right to Life Committee, "Supreme Court Decisions: Abortion." www.nrlc.org/Factsheets/FS16_SupremeCourt.pdf.

Pew Research Religion and Public Life Project, "A History of Key Abortion Rulings of the U.S. Supreme Court," January 16, 2013. www.pewforum.org/2013/01/16/a-history-of-key-abortion-rulings-of-the-us-supreme-court.

Pew Research Religion and Public Life Project, "*Roe v. Wade* at 40: Most Oppose Overturning Abortion Decision," January 16, 2013. www.pewforum.org/2013/01/16/roe-v-wade-at-40.

Adam Thomas, "Policy Solutions for Preventing Unplanned Pregnancy," Brookings Institution, March 2012. www.brookings.edu/research/reports/2012/03/unplanned-pregnancy-thomas.

Luisita Lopez Torregrosa, "In U.S., a Rekindled War Over Abortion," *New York Times*, June 25, 2013. www.nytimes.com/2013/06/26/us/26iht-letter26.html?ref=abortion.

Index

Note: Boldface page numbers indicate illustrations.

Picture Credits

Cover: iStockphoto.com

AP Images: 7, 13, 49, 78

Biophoto Associates/Science Photo Library: 33

© Bettmann/Corbis: 17

© Jerry Burch/Demotix/Corbis: 19

© Burger/Phanie Sarl/Corbis: 70

© Dave Kolpack/AP/Corbis: 44

© Science Picture Co./Corbis: 28

© Shannon Stapleton/Reuters/Corbis: 75

© Stringer/Reuters/Corbis: 55

Thinkstock Images: 61

About the Author

Carla Mooney is the author of many books for young adults and children. She lives in Pittsburgh, Pennsylvania, with her husband and three children.